Praise for RE-REGULATED

"Re-Regulated *is jam-packed with practical advice and tools
to begin to heal from dysregulation, disconnection, and self-defeating
behaviors. Bravely sharing her personal journey from the depths of despair,
Anna gifts us with her inspirational process of self-discovery
to overcome her own childhood trauma.*"

— **Dr. Nicole LePera**, author of the #1 *New York Times* bestsellers
How to Do the Work and *How to Be the Love You Seek*

"*Anna Runkle has not only crafted an easily accessible
and heartfelt resource for complex trauma, but she has also gifted the
reader with a system to work on self-regulation and practice. This is the
how-to that is often missing from the discussion of complex trauma,
and Anna delivers it with clarity and compassion.*"

— **Patrick Teahan**, childhood trauma educator,
YouTuber, and host of the *Our Whole Childhood* podcast

"*Anna Runkle's book* Re-Regulated *is a powerful guide to help people
who are dealing with major upheavals in their lives. Drawing on her own
traumatic childhood, she has developed a set of methods that can combat
depression, self-loathing, guilt, and self-defeating behaviors. Through
writing, meditation, and other exercises Runkle provides a strong
and supportive voice in providing a road map to better health.*"

— **James Pennebaker, Ph.D.**, professor emeritus of psychology at the
University of Texas at Austin and author of *Opening Up by Writing It Down*

"*Would you like to change the story of your life?
Anna Runkle gives you the tools and practices to transform wounds
into wisdom, pain into purpose, and fear into love.*"

— **Robert Holden**, author of *Shift Happens!*

"*Anna is truly one of the chainbreakers, those special people who refuse
to pass on generational trauma, and empathetically model to the rest of us
how we can do it too. Because of her journey of overcoming trauma, Anna
describes the hidden symptoms of trauma that so many can relate to. But
she takes it one step further and teaches practical steps to healing and
changing your life. . . . Re-Regulated is not like anything else out there—
a well-researched guide by someone who has lived through trauma,
recovered from its aftereffects, and then gone on to teach anyone who
needs it her practical approach to healing and changing your life.*"

— **Emma McAdam**, licensed marriage and family therapist
and founder of Therapy in a Nutshell

RE·REGULATED

Published in the United States by: Hay House LLC: www.hayhouse.com®
Published in Australia by: Hay House Australia Publishing Pty Ltd: www.hayhouse.com.au
Published in the United Kingdom by: Hay House UK Ltd: www.hayhouse.co.uk
Published in India by: Hay House Publishers (India) Pvt Ltd: www.hayhouse.co.in

Cover design: Micah Kandros • *Interior design:* Bryn Starr Best
Indexer: J S Editorial, LLC

Cataloging-in-Publication Data is on file at the Library of Congress

Hardcover ISBN: 978-1-4019-7863-1
E-book ISBN: 978-1-4019-7864-8
Audiobook ISBN: 978-1-4019-7865-5

10 9 8 7 6 5 4 3 2 1
1st edition, October 2024

Printed in the United States of America

This product uses responsibly sourced papers and/or recycled materials. For more information, see www.hayhouse.com.

RE·REGULATED

SET YOUR LIFE FREE FROM CHILDHOOD PTSD AND THE TRAUMA-DRIVEN BEHAVIORS THAT KEEP YOU STUCK

CREATOR OF THE CRAPPY CHILDHOOD FAIRY HEALING METHOD

ANNA RUNKLE

HAY HOUSE LLC
Carlsbad, California • New York City
London • Sydney • New Delhi

For all those who were once hurt and unseen,
and for the kind people who saw and helped us.

CONTENTS

INTRODUCTION

One night in the late winter of 1994, when I was 30 years old, I gave a ride to a woman I barely knew. Her name was Rachel. She had recently joined a theater group where I was a member, and she had no car. I volunteered to drive her home, which turned out to be a run-down old warehouse in a rough part of Oakland.

We sat talking in the car for a minute or two. She was telling me stories from when she'd lived on the streets and the hell she went through when she first got sober. Her arms were covered in tattoos, and she said the f-word or "f-ing" every sentence, about everything—even good things, even *God*. I didn't really believe in God then, but I liked her.

I had a secret, and when she was about to get out of the car, I said it out loud: I was thinking of ending my life the next day.

"Oh!" she said, as if it were a perfectly normal and understandable thing that people had told her a hundred times. She said she had something that might help me feel better and invited me to come inside and talk about it. So I said okay.

Thank God.

I was struggling at the time with what I now know was Childhood PTSD, but this wasn't a known "thing" back then. I'd sought help from my doctor and therapist, but their understanding of what was wrong and how to treat it left me feeling worse, not better. My life was going out of control.

Everything changed that night in Rachel's warehouse when she showed me a simple writing technique that immediately began to calm me. It set in motion a transformation in my life that unfolded quickly, even though I had no idea *why* the method I was using worked so well.

It would be 20 years before I learned the answer: I was *dysregulated*. Though it's only begun to be understood, neurological dysregulation is normal and common in people who were traumatized as children (as I was). It's the *core* symptom of Childhood PTSD, and it drives almost every other trauma symptom there is.

WHO CAN USE THIS BOOK

If you were abused or neglected or endured intense, ongoing stress in your childhood, it's likely you have some of the same symptoms I did. You may only be finding out now, as you read this book, that many of the struggles you've faced in your life are trauma related.

You've probably tried a dozen ways to heal and to function better. If you're like many of us, nothing you've tried has really helped. And because you haven't yet learned to re-regulate, the healing methods you've tried before (therapy, medication, groups, exercises, and so on) may even have made you feel worse.

The problem with healing trauma is that dysregulation makes it so hard to focus or get things done that doing the work of healing can seem impossible. But there's a better way to heal.

In this book, I'll teach you how to get *re-regulated*—what that feels like, how to do it quickly, and why staying regulated can help heal all the parts of your life: your health, relationships, emotions, and mental focus. Then I'll walk you through my radical step-by-step method for healing the life problems that tend to build up in the lives of people who are prone to dysregulation.

Much of what I'll be teaching you is common sense, though counterintuitive. You will recognize elements from other disciplines (neurobiology, psychology, the 12 Steps, traditional faiths), but the method is unlike anything you've tried before.

The science of trauma is advancing rapidly, and yet the culture of healing is slow to adopt new knowledge. Old assumptions and old modalities such as talk therapy and medication—long known to be only marginally effective—remain enshrined and calcified as

"The Way Trauma Should Be Treated." I am someone who didn't benefit from the standard approach, and like many people with classic trauma symptoms, I thought it was "just me."

When I did begin healing, the results were so dramatic that I quickly began sharing what I'd learned with anyone who wanted to heal too. Over the next 25 years, I taught hundreds of friends; then friends of friends; then groups; and eventually through my business, *Crappy Childhood Fairy*, which today has more than a million subscribers across platforms—offering videos, courses, webinars, workshops, coaching, and a friendly online community of people who use my method.

FIRST, LIFE HAD TO GET *REALLY* HARD

In a way, I'm glad things got as bad as they did for me; if they hadn't (assuming I survived), I'd still be dysregulated, stuck, sad, and alone—and just as terrified as I was on that night back in 1994 when I told Rachel the story of how hopeless I'd become.

A few weeks before that night, I'd been walking home from a coffee shop with a male friend. Four men in their late teens jumped out of a car, and one of them took a running leap and kicked my friend in the face, breaking his nose. One punched me in the temple and knocked me out, and then the whole group kicked me in the head and face several times, breaking my jaw and some teeth. In the middle of this, I came to and screamed, and they ran away. The cops swooped in and took us to the hospital. The next several weeks were a blur.

At this time, my mother had end-stage lung cancer. Just a week after the attack, I flew to Tucson for what I knew would be our last visit. I spent a few days at her bedside and then, when it was time to go, fumbled through an awkward good-bye. She sat cross-legged in her bed smoking a cigarette, looking at me while I sobbed and choked out the words that everything was okay, and I was sorry I was so angry at her all the time, and I loved her. She was pretty out of it and either couldn't or wouldn't say it back. My stepdad saw all this, and after a minute, the silence was getting weird. So I grabbed my suitcase and left to catch my plane.

Back home, my emotions were growing too intense. I'd already been gravely depressed for months after someone I'd deeply loved ended it with me for good. Now with the assault and the cold good-bye from my mother, I couldn't quite hold it together. A surge of grief, rage, and panic came over me, so intense my friends couldn't deal with me. At work (I was the marketing person for a chain of community clinics), I kept popping off with inappropriate and uncharacteristically hostile comments that almost got me fired.

Before my trauma storm, I'd been miserable, all right, but I'd functioned well enough. Now, just two months later, I couldn't focus my mind enough to read a full paragraph or dial a phone number. My emotions had gone rabid, and I couldn't hide how "crazy" I knew I seemed.

I asked Rachel the other day—we're still friends—if she thought I was crazy back then.

"Well, you were really freaked out," she told me. We were hanging out with a group of my students who were thrilled to meet the woman who first showed me the techniques that saved my life.

"Like . . . stressed?" I asked her.

"Like *batshit*," she said. Everyone laughed. They couldn't imagine me like that.

Back then, though, I was desperate. I needed help but couldn't find it.

My doctor at the time said my brain scan was "fine" and prescribed Xanax. My therapist said I needed to talk more about what had happened and had me increase my visits from once a week to three times a week.

They didn't know (because no one knew this then) that talk therapy and medication were likely to make my symptoms worse, not better.

And they did get worse. Much worse.

I was showing textbook signs of trauma—layer upon layer of trauma—from the recent assault to the lost relationships, and all the way back to abuse and neglect I'd endured as a child.

Like many other people with a rough childhood, I'd mostly "handled" what had happened to me and believed I was "tough." But the cluster of traumas so close together shattered the rickety compartmentalization I'd used to keep my childhood wounds contained. The genie was out of the bottle, and once the Childhood PTSD symptoms came out, I couldn't make them stop.

WHAT IS CHILDHOOD PTSD?

Childhood PTSD is the colloquial term for complex post-traumatic stress disorder (or CPTSD), a set of symptoms that can be caused by chronic exposure to intense stress, usually (but not always) during childhood (I'll explain this in detail in Chapter 1).

I grew up in a family riddled by alcoholism and addiction and all the problems that tend to go with that—violence, chaos, poverty, divorce, a lack of safety and supervision, and shame . . . so much shame.

When I was nine, my mother remarried and moved my siblings and me to Arizona. My father remained in California, where (if our VW bus was running) we'd visit him a couple of times a year. He was diagnosed with ALS when I was 13 and died two years later—crucial years in my development when I desperately needed a father. With scant adult support, I turned to boys and often stayed out all night, hoping real love would somehow blossom in these crude friends-with-benefits arrangements.

This pattern of attaching too quickly and holding on long past the expiration date of relationships stayed with me well into my 20s, along with the habit of overfunctioning—overworking and overstressing (with the help of coffee and lots and lots of cigarettes) to do enough and be enough to feel okay.

At the point when my healing began, I had been to 11 different therapists over 17 years, and of course we talked about my terrible childhood. But we seldom talked about my behavior and the ways my anger and impulsive romantic choices were causing me to be abandoned again and again.

I tried to do the work and spoke openly of what I was experiencing, hoping therapists would understand what was wrong and help me get my life on track.

You can feel it when someone really understands you. It's a relief that starts the healing process right away. I needed that badly, but I never got it in therapy or felt better, even a little. And now I know why.

Research suggests that for many people with early trauma, talk therapy can retrigger symptoms. That's certainly been the experience of many of us who've noticed the very act of talking about what happened can halt (or even reverse) healing that is already taking place. "For a hundred years or more, every textbook of psychology and psychotherapy has advised that some method of talking about distressing feelings can resolve them," says Dr. Bessel van der Kolk in his groundbreaking book, *The Body Keeps the Score*.[1] "However, as we've seen, the experience of trauma itself gets in the way of being able to do that. No matter how much insight and understanding we develop, the rational brain is basically impotent to talk the emotional brain out of its own reality."

Nonetheless, standard treatment protocols approved by insurers often limit patients to 10 sessions of talk therapy; if you don't improve (and if you have trauma symptoms, it's not likely you will), they'll put you on medication.

Talking about trauma can be one more trigger that causes your nervous system to slip into a dysregulated state. Your brain waves and body functions go slightly out of whack, and you get spaced out, emotionally overwhelmed, and unable to process information, among other things. Because of this, a significant proportion of people who were traumatized as kids haven't really benefited from therapy (if they even had access to it)—or they haven't benefited enough.

To add insult to injury, the medication prescribed to traumatized people can inhibit the *natural* ability to re-regulate, leaving them stuck in an unfocused and hyperemotional "loop," returning again and again to painful memories and dark (or pharmaceutically dampened) moods.

So I didn't get better. The more I talked about what I was feeling, the worse I felt. The more I tried to calm myself with prescribed medication, the more agitated I became.

During those terrible months after the assault, I'd call friends and monologue, trancelike, for 30 minutes, then realize I couldn't remember who I was talking to. I couldn't sleep and feared I was losing my mind—that I'd end up hospitalized or on the streets, and that even if help arrived, it couldn't help *me*. This was when I began to think I couldn't go on; I had come to believe I was not like other people—that I was unhelpable.

Then, finally, help arrived.

THE DAILY PRACTICE

What Rachel showed me in the wee hours of that night in 1994—a specific form of writing (a prayer of sorts)*—gave me immediate emotional relief. It is a way to express (or productively "vent") the fearful, resentful thoughts that run around our traumatized minds like hamsters on a wheel—and then to release them, or (according to what you believe) ask God to remove them.

When I first saw the format, it sounded so simple I didn't expect it to work. But I went home and wrote for over an hour, until I finally fell asleep. When I woke up, I couldn't wait to do the writing again. It felt *delicious* and relieved my chaotic thinking almost instantly. Soon, at Rachel's suggestion, I got trained to meditate (to rest my mind, she said), and I wrote, then meditated immediately afterward, morning and evening every day.

---

* The Daily Practice is not associated with 12-Step recovery, but it is derived from a 12-Step practice. The writing technique, and the suggestion to use Transcendental Meditation afterward, was shown to Rachel in the early 1990s by an old-timer in Alcoholics Anonymous named Sylvia D., who taught it to her as "the Daily Steps." Most people in AA don't work the Steps this way, but there are several hundred people with long-term sobriety (mostly in the U.S. and U.K.) who do. The 12-Step roots of the Daily Practice are described in more detail in Chapter 3 and in the Appendix.

I was still depressed at first, but every time I wrote and meditated, it gave way to a calm, sweet feeling. Very quickly, my depression lightened, and people noticed the change in me. Within two weeks, I had completely recovered my short-term memory and my mental focus, which I'd lost in the assault, and experienced a level of clarity, groundedness, and optimism I'd never known before. My life rocketed forward.

I came to call these techniques (writing and meditation) my "Daily Practice," and today it is the foundation of the healing method I teach, helping to re-regulate the nervous system and provide the clarity and insight needed for healing (you'll learn exactly how to do it in Chapter 3).

You might be skeptical about what I'm saying, and I think that's fair. *Another B.S. self-help thing* is what I thought when Rachel offered to teach me.

I'd put my faith in books and spiritual leaders and self-help programs before and gotten hopeful. Then always, after giving it a go, there was the cringe-y feeling that couldn't be ignored, certain to be followed by disappointment.

With the Daily Practice, the disappointment never came. Now it's 30 years later, and the techniques and principles I've adopted since then have proven sturdy and true.

HEALING BEGINS

At Rachel's suggestion, I began attending 12-Step groups for families of alcoholics and continued using my Daily Practice. I was soon mentoring women who asked to learn the techniques too. This helped to advance my own healing and my ability to speak to groups and work with others.

Even though I was healing, some of my dysfunctional behaviors were slow to change. I always felt "apart" from other people. I was usually single but had a series of shallow relationships with unworkable, unavailable, or uninterested men, leading only to trouble. One unhappy relationship was my brief first marriage, which (happily) led to the birth of my two beloved sons.

Being a divorced mother and working as an unbenefited free-lancer to pay the bills helped to put my problem into clear perspective: I could no longer allow troubled relationships to run my life. I didn't know what to do, or even what a healed life looked like exactly, but I *had* to find a way to do it.

In my 12-Step group, we defined our problem as "alcoholism in a friend or relative." I'd certainly had dozens of such friends and relatives and was affected, to be sure. But most of them had died or were no longer in my life, and my problem hadn't left with them.

I sought the help of several mentors from my career, recovery, and spiritual circles. I'd known for years that they had serious experience with moral transformation, but because the prospect scared me, I'd written them off as too directive and too judgy to trust with helping *me*.

Now, though, things were bad enough that I became open to guidance. I continued to read and to be of service to others, and most importantly, I took responsibility for my self-destructive patterns. There was something in *me*, and I knew instinctively that if I could find it and face it, I could fully heal. My life once again moved forward.

I first heard the term *Complex PTSD* when I read Pete Walker's *Complex PTSD: From Surviving to Thriving*, a seminal book that defines complex post-traumatic stress disorder (CPTSD) in practical terms anyone can understand. Also, in van der Kolk's work, I learned about the role of neurological dysregulation in driving CPTSD symptoms.

I'll cover this more deeply in subsequent chapters, but here's a quick primer on what CPTSD does: Early trauma can cause brain changes in children, and even in adulthood these can disturb the ordinary state of nervous-system regulation in brain waves, emotions, body systems, and cognitive processes. Anything that stresses a traumatized person can trigger dysregulation (in this book, the word *trigger* means a stimulus that activates dysregulation). In turn, dysregulation drives social disconnection and many other trauma symptoms and health problems that we had not previously realized were connected to trauma.

I am prone to dysregulation, I realized, thinking of how I was before I learned the Daily Practice and how I became whenever I didn't bother using it. Finally, I understood why I'd sometimes emotionally lash out under stress or lose my ability to stay on a schedule or use fine-motor coordination when new traumas (even small-ish ones) fell into my life. I had a name for it. It wasn't "just me."

Most people who had a chronically stressful childhood are prone to dysregulation. In me, this had generated a lifetime of "downstream" trauma-driven symptoms that I had, until that day, believed were personal failings. I thought I was just mean, lazy, reckless, or too damaged to pull my life together. But I was wrong (well, mostly wrong!). I had CPTSD.

I learned that all I'd done in therapy—the focus on other people and on what happened in the past—was not really therapeutic in my case. Rather, my problem—and the potential for healing—was in *me*, in *present time.*

I had the remedy in my hands at last—the Daily Practice to regulate my nervous system so that healing became possible, plus the willingness to change the trauma-driven behaviors that had, until then, continually pushed me *back* into dysregulation.

I couldn't wait to share the news with every traumatized person I knew: "It's called dysregulation! It's a neurological injury! It's *not our fault!*"

I tell you this in such detail because I want you to know as plainly as I know now: Many of your struggles are just normal symptoms for people who grew up with abuse and neglect. It's no *wonder* you've struggled with simple things like paying attention, being on time, or feeling at ease in a group. No wonder, with your family history and everything your parents failed to teach you, that so many things have been so hard.

When I first understood I have CPTSD, I was standing in our bedroom, holding Pete Walker's book in my hands. I ran yelling from the room, calling out for my husband (my *now* husband, who is wonderful), laughing and crying at the same time. The shame I'd carried all my life fell off my shoulders like a heavy cloak.

The techniques alone had helped me master re-regulation. Once I learned the nature of Complex PTSD, I was able to quickly add action steps and principles that allowed me to transform the behavior patterns that were still holding me back.

THE BIRTH OF CRAPPY CHILDHOOD FAIRY

The method I teach for healing trauma symptoms was developed over 30 years (and I continue to refine it to this day). First I healed myself, and then I shared with others, one-on-one and in living-room gatherings. In 2016, I had so many requests to teach the method that in the spirit of efficiency, I launched the blog *Crappy Childhood Fairy* so I could write the instructions down and share a link with anyone who sought my help. I was still flooded with requests and questions, so I made a video for the blog, teaching the technique in detail, and hosted it on YouTube. I added more posts and videos to teach the sequence of steps as my healing method developed. To my surprise, the videos quickly eclipsed the blog in terms of subscribers, drawing strangers from all over the world. Soon I turned the Daily Practice into an online course and then added more courses and a membership program, and eventually I hired a team to help me manage it all.

Until the pandemic hit in 2020, I did all this in my "spare" time. When the lockdown began, I dropped my career (by this time I owned a corporate video-production company) and began working full time as "The Fairy," producing YouTube videos and building courses, webinars, and coaching programs and later, live workshops, retreats, and a podcast.

Today I reach millions of people with my message of encouragement and a practical path of healing that anyone can follow, whether they have access to professional help or not.

My mission is to change the paradigm of trauma healing—away from the notion that experts have the answers and you depend on *them*—and toward the knowledge that *you* are sovereign over your healing. By this I mean that you are the ruler of your destiny and the decisions that take you there. *You* are the one who will identify your symptoms, seeking the counsel of experts (if you wish) and working day-to-day, in real time, to transform your life. I believe this is a better and more empowered approach to healing.

If treatments you've tried in the past haven't worked, don't give up, because what I'm going to show you is a *new* approach that may help *you*. If you can calm even one or two trauma symptoms, this could be enough to prevent problems that used to derail your life and to change everything for the better.

I am here to share a wider vision of what's possible for people like you and me, and to help all those I can to heal and lead lives of joy and purpose. Healing from trauma is the most life-changing thing we can do, and it's the path that empowers us to truly make a difference in the world.

I invite you to open your mind to the possibility that you may be capable of faster, more thorough healing than you thought possible—and that, rather than being helpless to change, you have the power to *heal yourself*. In this book, I'll teach you how to do it.

The chapters are laid out in the sequence that is necessary to learn and integrate each step of my method. Because each lesson builds your capacity to do the work of the *next* chapter, I recommend you work through each chapter in order. You'll find checklists, questions, worksheets, and assignments in the chapters too, and these will help you adopt the lessons in your day-to-day life.

First, I'll teach you the basics about Complex PTSD and help you clarify the ways your trauma affected and is still affecting you, and why writing about negative thoughts in the Daily Practice (which you'll learn in Chapter 3) can be more helpful than talking about them.

I'll shed light on some common treatments you may have tried (or may yet try), including traditional, cognitive-based and body-based modalities and how they are similar or different to the method you'll learn in this book.

I'll teach you about neurological dysregulation—what it feels like, what triggers it, and how to re-regulate as quickly as possible. I'll also walk through some common manifestations of *emotional* dysregulation, which, left untreated, can ruin relationships; I'll teach you to bring intense reactions under control and repair conflicts instead.

I'll help you recognize the role of dysregulation in causing you to feel disconnected from others for so much of your life and how you can rebuild your capacity to have the close, fulfilling relationships you deserve. Dysregulation also drives the self-defeating behaviors that are common in traumatized people, and I'll help you begin the process of healing them too.

Finally, I'll show you how to discover the unique gifts that will allow you to become your full and real self. This, after all, is the real goal of healing.

WHAT YOU'LL NEED TO DO THIS WORK

- A JOURNAL. This is a sturdy or bound notebook that you'll keep together with this book, to make notes about what you're learning and choosing to incorporate in your healing work. Be careful to keep it private. You'll be answering journal prompts placed throughout each chapter of the book, inviting you to reflect on the lessons and apply them to your daily life.

- A SCRATCH PAD. This is what you'll use to do the Daily Practice writing technique twice a day. After each writing session, you'll shred the pages and throw them away. The paper doesn't need to be fancy, and you won't be rereading it.

- A PEN OR PENCIL.

There are resources available online that you can use, download, and print if you like, to support your work in the book. Go to **re-regulated.com**.

Like everyone, you need and deserve to feel happier and to shed your old cloak of shame and pessimism. Your real happiness is waiting for you to step up and become all you were meant to be—bringing all that you have to share with a world that desperately needs you.

You may not know yet how you'll heal, but it's not necessary to know. You only need to get started. I'm here to tell you with certainty: **Healing is possible**.

Let's begin!

CHAPTER 1

THE TRUTH ABOUT CHILDHOOD TRAUMA

By now, I trust you are sensing a cause for *hope* and feel excited to begin the path. Healing really is possible, no matter what you've tried or what has disappointed you in the past. New progress begins when you understand what Complex PTSD *is,* and the role played by dysregulation in driving so many of its symptoms.

You probably either suspect or *know* that traumatic events when you were a child are still having a negative impact on you today. You may be wondering what's merely part of your personality and what might count as "real" CPTSD.

There is a mountain of evidence that early trauma, especially abuse and neglect, causes lasting harm. But in the clinical literature, a specific set of symptoms is not consistently defined, and no screening or treatment protocols have been widely adopted. So even though hundreds of millions of people worldwide are estimated to have CPTSD, most of us have never been formally diagnosed. In this chapter, I'll teach you some of the common symptoms of CPTSD and what we know about them. I'll need to get a bit technical to explain the science of trauma. This is so you can truly know, in your mind and heart, that the symptoms you've experienced are normal, and not your fault.

WHY AREN'T MORE PEOPLE DIAGNOSED?

As a diagnosis, CPTSD is not yet recognized in the Diagnostic Statistical Manual (DSM) used in the United States, but it was recently added to the latest edition of the World Health Organization's International Classification of Diseases (ICD-11), with many calls to advance clinical understanding of the causes, symptoms, and treatments for it.

According to the National Institutes of Health (NIH), CPTSD affects 1 to 8 percent of the world's population.[1] This is a wide variance that reflects inconsistent diagnostic criteria and poor systems for patient evaluation. Few clinicians have sufficient knowledge of symptoms to even recognize CPTSD, let alone know what to do for patients they screen who tick all the boxes.

In addition, providers and other experts disagree on (or misunderstand) how CPTSD is distinct from "regular" PTSD, and misdiagnoses (including dismissing symptoms as "just stress" or "all in your head") are common.

Even if these practitioners know what CPTSD is, most are unclear about diagnostic criteria that distinguish it from things like borderline personality disorder, ADHD, anxiety, or depression, which each have some overlapping symptoms with CPTSD but are not the same.

A 2019 study has shown that practitioners' beliefs about what each diagnosis means and how it should be treated vary *so* much as to be almost meaningless,[2] and further, most diagnoses mask the role of trauma in causing those symptoms in the first place.

This doesn't have to stop us from healing, though. We don't need the approval of experts to get started with naming our problems and healing our lives. The healing method I'll be teaching you in this book can be helpful with or without a diagnosis and with or without professional help. My approach is focused less on the *causes* of your trauma (harm that people did to you in the past) and more on the *symptoms* that are affecting you now. When you learn to notice and manage those symptoms, real change becomes possible, and you can live a happier, more stable, and more connected life.

WHAT'S THE DIFFERENCE BETWEEN PTSD, COMPLEX PTSD (CPTSD), AND CHILDHOOD PTSD?

PTSD, or post-traumatic stress disorder, is a clinical diagnosis usually applied in cases where people had a traumatic event happen in adulthood—taking part in a battle or being in a car accident, for example. The symptoms might include flashbacks, anxiety, depression, hypervigilance (always keeping an eye out for danger), insomnia, withdrawing from people, or exploding emotionally sometimes.

Another, second kind of PTSD is Complex PTSD (abbreviated as CPTSD), which is caused by chronic, ongoing exposure to emotional or physical trauma—things such as living through a long war, being in a violent relationship, or growing up neglected, abused, or otherwise intensely stressed.

CPTSD can develop in response to trauma later in life, but most people who have it developed it in childhood. The symptoms are in many ways similar to PTSD, but can involve additional injury to emotional and nervous-system regulation, one's sense of identity, and the ability to form and keep relationships.

What I teach can be helpful no matter when you became traumatized, but because early trauma has a unique potential to affect your developing brain and nervous system, it's a little different from adult-onset CPTSD, and it's where my work is focused.

You will hear me say both "CPTSD" (where the *C* stands for "complex") and "Childhood PTSD," which is a colloquial term for the kind of CPTSD that developed during childhood. These are imprecise terms, but I trust that as I'm teaching, you will freely apply the lessons to yourself when you feel they fit.

DO YOU HAVE CHILDHOOD PTSD? HERE ARE SOME SIGNS

People who were abused or neglected in childhood often have a common pattern of symptoms; however, these don't *always* indicate that trauma has happened, and they're a little different in each person.

This list of questions can't provide you with a diagnosis, but it asks about common "palpable" symptoms (the ones you feel and see). If you identify even a few of them as something you regularly experience, it may be that past trauma is the cause.

Whether or not you know *why* you have the symptoms, you can recognize them and begin working on them right away; in the coming chapters, I'll show you how.

As you read these questions, keep count of how many of the mentioned signs you've noticed in yourself. There are no right or wrong answers.

- Have you had depression, anxiety, or other mental health problems?

- Do you have trouble setting boundaries or saying no?

- Do you feel that you are unexplainably separate from other people and groups?

- Have you damaged your relationships or your career because of intense emotions or outbursts of sadness, jealousy, panic, or anger when it didn't seem appropriate?

- Does the fear of being alone cause you to stay in relationships you can't stand?

- Do you have more than your share of conflict with your partner, family, friends, and co-workers?

- Do you find people so triggering that you end up avoiding social situations?

- Do you feel that you "attract" unavailable, destructive, or abusive people?

- Do you smoke cigarettes or use food, alcohol, or drugs in an addictive way?

- Is physical clutter a problem for you?

- Do you tend to "space out" at odd times, struggling to be productive and focused?

- Do you get clumsy at seemingly random times, tripping over things or dropping things?

- When you're trying to do something familiar (especially when you're hurrying or under pressure), do you sometimes get too flustered to function?

- Do you constantly feel overwhelmed because of all you have to get done?

- Do you struggle to get much of anything done, falling behind on responsibilities, bills, or important communication?

- Do you have unexplained health problems that seem to have no clear cause?

FOR YOUR JOURNAL
• • • • • • • •

HERE ARE QUESTIONS FOR YOU TO ANSWER IN YOUR JOURNAL (YOU'LL FIND SIMILAR JOURNAL PROMPTS THROUGHOUT THE BOOK). TOGETHER, THE QUESTIONS IN THIS BOOK WILL HELP YOU IDENTIFY THE WAYS PAST TRAUMA HAS AFFECTED YOU AND PLAN NEXT STEPS FOR YOUR HEALING. REMEMBER TO KEEP YOUR JOURNAL PRIVATE SO IT'S A SAFE PLACE TO WRITE YOUR THOUGHTS AND EXPERIENCES.

- How many of the symptoms listed above have you experienced?
- Which have affected your life the most?
- Are there some you didn't know were associated with trauma?

WHAT DO YOUR *YES* ANSWERS MEAN?

Each symptom in the list is a symptom that's common for people who were abused and neglected as children. They include problems with emotions, behaviors, and relationships, as well as cognitive and physiological functioning. If you were traumatized as a child and you had a lot of *yes* answers in this quiz, please know that you're not broken. *These symptoms are a normal response to abnormal experiences and circumstances during childhood.*

The second thing to know is, you didn't cause these symptoms. You may have blamed yourself and attacked yourself as lazy, dumb, needy, selfish, or crazy (or maybe other people called you these things). But trauma can produce these symptoms in almost anyone, even animals. (Have you ever met a shelter dog who had been abandoned or mistreated and who trembled and cowered, even when a kind person tried to help? You would never think to blame the dog.) In the same way, you are not to blame. You didn't ask for neglect or abuse, and you definitely didn't deserve it.

It's instinctive to feel (as many of us have felt) that *someone* should fix what happened—that it can and ought to be set right. It's rare that parents or others who traumatized us acknowledge what they did, let alone try to repair the damage. If (hypothetically) they did, your relationship might improve, and that would be good. But the neurological injury from the original trauma has already happened. This means that your symptoms will tend to persist no matter what other people do.

It's *what you do* that changes things. You can read scientific research and consult with trauma experts, but it is *you* who will heal yourself. I urge you not to wait until you know exactly what happened in the past or until you find the perfect therapist and get a diagnosis. Instead, you can use this book to build your knowledge about childhood trauma, identify the ways it has affected you, and get started with your healing.

Don't be discouraged just because your past efforts haven't worked. Everything you've tried in the past counts as a data point, as research. But this is different.

What I'm going to show you is a *new* approach. If you follow my instructions, you may find that some of your symptoms resolve quickly and easily. Other symptoms may take time and practice. But ask yourself: If even half of the symptoms you have now could be healed—or if they could be even *halfway* healed—would it make a difference in your life?

I'm willing to bet that a 50 percent improvement in even one of the symptoms could make it possible for transformation around the other symptoms, and in every part of your life.

WHY HAVE YOU NEVER HEARD ABOUT THESE SYMPTOMS BEFORE?

Many medical and mental-health professionals have received training that qualifies them to say their work is "trauma informed," but unfortunately, this can mean anything from a two-hour workshop to a two-year certification program—and even then, there's little agreement about what helps people.

Most treatment protocols are still organized around a few outdated ideas that have dominated the way childhood trauma has been viewed for decades. But it turns out (and this is good news) they aren't completely true.

It's good news because it explains why so many of us (myself included) spent years of our lives trying to get help for trauma-related symptoms and getting too little improvement, or no improvement at all. It's not because we were failures. It's because practitioners didn't know yet about Childhood PTSD.

You may have tried the methods like therapy and medication and groups that you were told would work—methods that worked so well for other people but that didn't help *you*, not really.

It turns out the role of the nervous system is the *big* missing piece in conventional trauma treatment, and this could be why you felt like you were stuck on a healing treadmill, getting nowhere. Knowing the truth will liberate your understanding, and just might save your life.

IT'S NOT IN YOUR MIND:
WHAT THE EXPERTS GOT WRONG

Until recently, the medical and mental-health world believed the impact of early trauma on adults was primarily *psychological*, involving thoughts, feelings, and how you behave. We now know that a big part of the impact is also *neurological*. Childhood trauma can injure brain and nervous-system development, causing major disruption to your cognitive and physiological functioning, which in turn can influence every part of your mind, your emotions, your body, and your choices in life.

This is a completely different understanding from what everyone used to believe, and it has profound implications about symptoms and treatment. It also explains why so many of us have failed to respond to psychologically oriented treatments and why, despite wanting to live happily, we keep finding ourselves stuck in dysfunctional patterns and self-defeating behaviors. From the lens of psychology, that looks like a *choice*, even if unconscious.

For example, if you've had a pattern of unhappy relationships with emotionally unavailable people, you may have been told by those experts, "You're just trying to re-create your childhood." I literally used to feel ashamed that I didn't understand how this could be true, when I wanted (like everyone else) to be happy and loved. But I'd pretend, and go along with it, and hope that admitting such an ugly desire would illuminate a path to healing.

It never did, because it wasn't true. And now we know: There are dozens of ways that past trauma pushes us into repeating negative patterns, but *wanting* to re-create a terrible childhood isn't one of them.

Once again, the culprit is the nervous system, and in the coming chapters I'll explain how that plays out. You're not "trying" to have a bad relationship any more than you're "trying" to have a migraine. Bad relationships and migraines (though they could happen to anyone) are both part of CPTSD's symptom pattern, and they are both influenced, sometimes driven, by the nervous-system irregularities associated with trauma.

Of course we are psychologically affected by early trauma, but the root of our lingering trauma symptoms is neurological. As Bessel van der Kolk has said, "It's not in your mind. *It's in your brain.*"

So, how do we know this?

A BREAKTHROUGH

The long-term effects of childhood trauma got onto the radar back in the mid '90s with a big research project called the ACE study. It's become an accepted (if imperfect) way to measure the scope of a person's early trauma and to predict how it might affect them throughout their life.

The ACE study began when Dr. Vincent Felitti of Kaiser Permanente and Dr. Robert Anda of the U.S. Centers for Disease Control and Prevention interviewed hundreds of study participants about their history of what the doctors called "adverse childhood experiences." They created a survey with 10 questions about bad things that might have happened to you when you were a kid. You get one point for each question where you answer yes, and so your score would be somewhere between 0 and 10.

The questions have to do with physical abuse, sexual abuse, emotional abuse, physical neglect, emotional neglect, witnessing your mother being treated violently, household substance abuse, mental illness, parental separation or divorce, and incarceration of a family member. Of course, there are dozens of other experiences that could be included, such as seeing your father abused, the death of a parent, being desperately poor, living as a refugee, or being subjected to racism, bullying, or ostracization. You can take this into consideration if you decide to take the test, which you can do at **re-regulated.com**.

The researchers found that the higher your ACE score, the higher the probability that you'll experience certain problems in your life. These include things you'd expect to see as a matter of common sense, such as depression, anxiety, addictions, and troubled relationships. But the study also delivered some surprises. It showed clearly that early trauma is closely correlated with a higher incidence of serious chronic diseases and stress-related disorders.

It's important to remember that these symptoms reflect an elevated *probability* of risk that you'll experience these symptoms, but not a certainty. The healing work you're doing now, and in the rest of this book, are constructive steps that can reduce your risk by calming dysregulation.

Physiological problems correlated with a high ACE score:

- Migraines
- Gastrointestinal disorders like irritable bowel syndrome
- Increased reproductive disorders like endometriosis, pelvic inflammatory disease
- Obesity
- Metabolic disorder and diabetes
- Heart disease
- Cancer
- Chronic lung disease
- Hypertension and stroke
- Autoimmune diseases like thyroid disorders, multiple sclerosis, rheumatoid arthritis, chronic fatigue, lupus, vitiligo
- Increased infections
- Fibromyalgia and chronic pain

The implications of these findings are *huge*, making it clear that trauma produces something even more widespread than just psychological wounds. Since the ACE study was first published, researchers have identified an even wider range of problems (physical, cognitive, behavioral, and psychological) that are caused or exacerbated by trauma. Only one thing could affect so many physiological functions: the nervous system.

Many medical and mental-health providers know and acknowledge the role of trauma and its impact on the nervous system as important drivers of many (if not most) medical and mental-health problems. It may take them decades to fully integrate this knowledge into the way they care for patients. What those of us with CPTSD can do now is notice the symptoms that have resulted from our own trauma wounds and then set to work—independently or with help from peers and professionals—on healing them.

Our work begins by learning the wider range of problems known to be associated with a history of trauma in childhood.

THE LASTING WOUNDS OF CHILDHOOD PTSD

The signs of trauma are like an octopus; they show up in different parts of your life but are connected to one central injury. In this section, I'll list some of the symptom patterns associated with abuse and neglect in your childhood. You may have some but not all of them.

Most of the symptoms are not exclusively connected to trauma. They *could* happen to anyone. But there are four distinctive markers that I call "hallmarks" because they are exceptionally common in traumatized people, they are potentially damaging, and most other trauma symptoms begin with one of them. They are: neurological dysregulation, negative self-talk, emotional dysregulation, and emotional flashbacks.

The Four Hallmark Symptoms of CPTSD

Neurological Dysregulation

Because it is the *core* symptom that drives most other CPTSD symptoms, neurological dysregulation is the first and most important thing to heal. *Neurological dysregulation* refers to a shift in your nervous-system function that can cause many normal functions to become disrupted (brain waves, heartbeat, hormone secretions, and even thought processes, for example), slightly altering their normal rhythm—with surprisingly pervasive consequences.

Everyone gets dysregulated sometimes, and most people eventually get re-regulated. With Childhood PTSD, however, we can get dysregulated more easily and stay dysregulated more of the time. These long spans of time when we're dysregulated are when many of our other symptoms—physical, emotional, and behavioral—take root.

Dysregulation begins with a *trigger*—a thought, memory, or experience (getting criticized, for example) that hits the nervous system and produces an "out of sync" response. Some aspects of dysregulation can be felt, including overly intense emotions, numbness in your face or hands, or feeling flustered or spaced out.

Dysregulation is often the culprit in less palpable symptoms too—for example, when you struggle to put words together, remember, or focus on tasks. Dysregulation gets activated when you're confronted with stressors and crises and can blind you to red flags or propel you into making mistakes (sometimes the same ones you've made many, many times). Just when action is needed, it can create a kind of mental chaos or put you in a frozen trance.

It's also believed to be the mechanism by which past trauma alters important physiological processes, causing compromised immune function and chronic disease and pain states, often without a detectable organic cause.

Whether dysregulation is depressing your mood, making you sick, trapping you in brain fog, or making social interactions too triggering to manage, it is central to virtually all other trauma symptoms.

Most people, including many medical and mental-health practitioners, don't know about dysregulation (especially its neurological manifestations). You may have been trying for years to engage in healing methods *while* dysregulated, and this is a big reason why you may have had limited benefit. I'll help you deepen your understanding of neurological dysregulation in Chapter 4, and the triggers that set it off in Chapter 5.

Negative Self-Talk

Everyone engages in negative self-talk to some degree, but because the neurological injury of CPTSD can make it hard to process your thoughts, feelings, and memories, mental chatter can get "backed up" in your mind and tends to turn negative. The thoughts, generally involving anger and anxiety, can destroy your focus, distort your perception, and keep you from being emotionally present enough to sustain healthy relationships with people. Instead of waking up refreshed and open to the day, you may find negative self-talk fills your mind with anxious, angry thoughts that begin immediately to clutter your thinking.

This is why the Daily Practice is such an important part of my approach to healing; the negative mental chatter limits your self-awareness and blocks your ability to think clearly. Before I've written each morning, my thoughts go something like this: *Oh for God's sake. Is it morning? Ugh. Everything hurts, and I'm hot. I probably look awful. I don't want to get up. Where's the cat? Oh, there she is. I wonder whatever happened to those two women I used to have lunch with on Wednesdays. They hate me. Ouch, sat on my pencil. Well, I never liked them anyway. What a couple of self-righteous . . . Hey! What's that noise? Oh, the cat must've jumped down off the bed. Those women are only interested in gossip. Why did I try so hard to make them like me? I always do that. Oops, where's my slipper?* (And so on.)

The Daily Practice functions as a system to move those negative, unprocessed thoughts "downstream," leaving you with a little mental and emotional space inside to be responsive to the demands of the present hour. I'll teach you exactly how to do the Daily Practice in Chapter 3.

Emotional Dysregulation

Driven by a complex interaction between the amygdala, hippocampus, hypothalamus, and prefrontal cortex, your brain's emotional responses can vary from *way* too strong to almost totally flat, without feeling to *you* like anything is odd.

Emotional dysregulation is, for some people, always there. For others, it's a reaction to specific triggers like abandonment, feeling trapped, or being criticized or excluded. You might rage and lash out, freak out with fear, cry uncontrollably over something small, or all the above. Sometimes these outward expressions of dysregulation are followed by a spell of emotional "flatness," when you've functionally short-circuited and lapsed into an emotionless dissociation.

With CPTSD, the reaction can be so strong and so physical that in the moments leading to an emotional outburst, you can almost feel the stress hormones running through your body. These extreme emotional states can be devastating to your relationships with partners, friends, family members, and co-workers. For many people with CPTSD, it costs them everything.

You will learn in Chapter 6 how to notice emotional dysregulation and halt any harmful behaviors while you get re-regulated, ready to repair and resume the communication you were trying to have.

Emotional Flashbacks

One phenomenon that particularly marks CPTSD is *emotional flashbacks*, a term coined by the therapist and author Pete Walker. It's good to have a name for the tide of brutal emotions that can come over you suddenly at odd times, bringing out your worst trauma-driven behaviors. Though it often *feels* as if events or people have triggered the bad feelings, an emotional flashback is a nonvisual reliving of traumatic experiences when you were small that is unconnected to present-day events.

A person with CPTSD will flood (that's what it's called: *flooding*) with an overwhelming sense of grief, panic, and rage—or all those feelings at once. It can happen when you wake up (as it sometimes does for me) or when something triggers you. It can even happen in response to a positive trigger, like receiving a present. You're not reliving some childhood experience consciously; you know that you are here in present time. But the emotions don't know it, and so you're reacting as you did during the older trauma, especially if it happened before you could speak or form conscious memories.

These flashbacks sometimes appear to be bad moods out of nowhere, or just plain old emotional dysregulation. But emotional flashbacks are more specific, sucking you into an old response to an experience that's no longer happening. Flashbacks can alter your perceptions of whom you can trust and who is to blame for your pain. They can prompt you to say hurtful things and act impulsively, damaging relationships and ruining opportunities. If you can learn to stop them, you can prevent great harm that you'd have otherwise caused.

Flashbacks tend to have a theme, and once you know your theme(s), it's possible to recognize flashbacks *while* you're having them.

My theme is "I have to do *everything* around here." This likely comes from being neglected and actually having to do everything for myself when I was small, but that's not what I'm *thinking* during a flashback. In my mind, my terrible mood is because *present-day* people are doing this to me. Even if there's a little bit of truth in what's bothering me, the ragged feeling of overwhelm and despair (and the startled look in other people's eyes at how intense I'm being) is how I know a flashback is happening. Recognizing it is half the battle.

One particularly harsh kind of flashback is called *abandonment mélange* (again coined by Pete Walker). It's common in people who were emotionally or physically neglected—or literally abandoned—in childhood. Triggered by rejection, a breakup, or even thoughts that a loved one might be pulling away, this reaction involves a toxic mix of rage, grief, despair, and fear far above the level most people would experience. It can feel like you've been cast out of the human race or out of the world, and it's driven many of us back to unhappy and even dangerous relationships that we wanted desperately to leave. After the good feeling of freedom brought on by leaving, the mélange comes like a wave of pain that makes leaving feel unbearable after all. As with other forms of emotional flashback, recognizing that you're "in" an abandonment mélange can help to immediately reduce its intensity so you can better move forward with solid tools for ongoing healing and change.

More Symptom Patterns
Associated with Childhood Trauma

Difficulty with Relationships

The wounds of trauma can drive us to attach too quickly to others we barely know, often resulting in relationships with people who are troubled, emotionally unavailable, or abusive. Abandonment trauma compels us to cling too tightly to friends and to stay in relationships where we aren't loved or treated well. Some of us manifest trauma as an avoidance of relationships altogether, finding interactions with people to be too overwhelming or painful to bear.

In addition, emotional dysregulation can generate instability and conflict in relationships with friends, co-workers, partners, and family. Under stress, you may "go from 0 to 60" emotionally. You may react with *fury* when others would merely feel angry, or you *panic* when others might feel slightly worried. If you're like most people with Childhood PTSD, this has damaged relationships with people you love and value dearly, and it may have cost you good jobs or advancement and opportunities for fun and personal growth.

Significantly Higher Rates of
Psychological and Mood Problems

Compared to the general population, those of us who grew up abused or neglected are especially prone to depression and anxiety. This may be an understandable response to painful memories and consequences of trauma-driven behavior, but there may also be a neurological component stemming from the brain changes in our early development. People traumatized as children also have an increased incidence of mental illness such as bipolar disorder as well as personality disorders such as borderline personality and narcissistic personality.

Higher Incidence of Cognitive Difficulties

People with Childhood PTSD are more likely than others to have learning disabilities and to be diagnosed with ADHD (though some experts believe that many ADHD cases are in fact Complex PTSD, which may be easier to treat and heal). We are more likely than others to have memory problems and have a higher incidence of dementia.

Many of us labor under a chronic state of mental overwhelm. Since trauma can injure our ability to process thoughts and emotions, the introduction of new experiences or the need to organize and act upon new information can feel like too much. Outward signs of this include procrastination, clutter, and difficulty making decisions.

Increased Prevalence of High-Risk Behaviors

Childhood trauma is correlated with an impaired ability to predict the relative risk involved in one decision versus another. Under pressure, the reasoning centers of the brain become less active at the same time emotional centers are going into high gear.

Those of us who grew up abused or neglected are more likely than the general population to use nicotine, drugs, and alcohol, with significantly higher rates of addiction (which may be partly hereditary). We are more likely to develop eating disorders.

On average we have a higher number of sexual partners than other people, and (particularly if we were sexually abused) are more likely to be sexually assaulted as adults. Because we are prone to emotional dysregulation and "checking out" in stressful situations (and our relationships tend to be stressful), we have higher-than-average rates of unintended pregnancy as well as abortion.

We are more likely to be violent toward other people and to be victims of violence. We are more likely to feel suicidal or to attempt suicide.

Poverty and Limited Career Advancement

Without a doubt, trauma can hold people back in terms of money and career. First, the family culture and home environment can limit your education and your ability to learn or to envision a path toward a successful future. Dysregulation, social difficulties, self-defeating behaviors, and ongoing crises can ruin opportunities and block you from trying for them in the first place.

These are just some of the common manifestations of trauma in our lives. Finally, it is recognized that trauma in childhood can play a significant role in not just the development of psychological and behavioral problems, but of *physiological* and *neurological* problems too. And what this means is that learning to heal Childhood PTSD is one of the most life-changing things we can do as individuals and as a society.

But it raises the question: What is the *mechanism* by which trauma does all this damage?

HOW EARLY TRAUMA INJURES THE NERVOUS SYSTEM

When you're a baby or small child, trauma is especially toxic for the developing brain (this is why CPTSD is sometimes called *developmental trauma*). Abuse or neglect can cause nervous-system changes, especially around emotional processing and the body's natural response to stress. And while physical and sexual abuse are understood by virtually everyone to be gravely harmful, emotional neglect (in many cases) appears to be at least as damaging to kids.

For healthy brain development, a child needs parents to connect with them, mirror them, make eye contact and talk to them, and to respond to their feelings, needs, and accomplishments. This is exactly what is missing in the lives of children who are neglected.

Whether from abuse or neglect (or both), the child's brain development is slowed and altered. They can become overwhelmed by stress and all the physiological reactions (such as a release of adrenaline) that come with that, which is called *hyperarousal*.

The child might develop a more or less permanent state of terror that they'll be left alone or hurt again (hypervigilance), or they'll learn to escape unbearable situations by just spacing out, seeming to need nothing (dissociation).

Neglected children sometimes develop a tendency to imagine love where there is no love, entrenching themselves in a world of maladaptive daydreaming or fantasy that will complicate every part of their later life.

The child now has what amounts to a neurological "injury," which can generate lifelong difficulties—emotional, psychological, cognitive, and physical—that only recently have come to be understood as trauma symptoms.

Cognitive and behavioral symptoms in children include things like not being able to connect with people, sit still or pay attention, control impulses, and, of course, learn.

Physical symptoms begin to appear as well, including headaches and digestive problems, sleep disturbances, bed-wetting, asthma, fatigue, overeating or not being able to eat enough, nervous tics like skin picking, and, in some cases as the child gets older, early onset of puberty. Gradually, the same symptoms adults experience begin to appear too.

But trauma isn't the only thing that shapes us. Resilience factors and positive experiences play a strong role too, sometimes mitigating the worst damage that trauma could otherwise have caused (this is one reason that trauma in the family impacts siblings differently). Resilience factors include personality traits such as a positive outlook, a sense of competence and self-efficacy, and taking an interest in activities (such as sports or the arts) where skills and connections can be developed. Supportive adults from outside the family (teachers, coaches, relatives, or neighbors) can powerfully influence a child's resilience too.

WHAT HAPPENED TO YOU?

If you've tried any other approach to healing trauma before, there was probably a strong emphasis on telling your *story*—talking about what happened, who did it, how you felt about it, and how you feel about it now.

It's important to tell your story and to acknowledge how you were harmed. But in my approach to healing, this is not what we emphasize. It's something we write down early in the healing process so that we can face the past. This can be useful as we do the work of identifying and healing symptoms. It also helps to see with certainty that the abuse and neglect we suffered in childhood was not our fault. We didn't ask for it, and we could not help becoming affected by it.

But old traumas have a way of preoccupying us—like a chipped tooth that you can't resist touching with the tip of your tongue, even though it's sharp and it hurts. You may have been conditioned to keep your focus on hurtful things that happened in the past, because in the mental-health world, they used to believe that *more* focus was what would someday heal you. But in my method, you may find that *less* focus on the past is how you discover your most powerful healing opportunity—within yourself, *right now.*

Old traumas are bound to pop up in your mind, and as we progress through the steps of your healing, I will teach you to hold those thoughts and memories lightly. You don't have to suppress them or go into denial about them, but instead of *speaking* about them, you're encouraged to pour them onto the page when you begin to use the Daily Practice techniques. Here they can be processed and moved "downstream," which drains their power to distract and control you in your life today.

If you choose to do the Acknowledging What Happened exercise, I encourage you to make it a quick step. The work you'll be doing through the rest of this book is where your ongoing healing will happen. This part, naming what happened to cause your trauma, sets the stage.

ACKNOWLEDGING WHAT HAPPENED

Even if you've been in therapy before, you may never have written down in one place the experiences that traumatized you. Here you will list what happened, followed by ways you think these events may have affected you, then and now.

Not every traumatic event in the past is still affecting you, and if something isn't, there's no need to write it down. But here is where you're invited to consider the problems that have lingered, or where a new symptom has appeared that you feel originates from an earlier trauma.

In your journal, draw three columns (or answer the three questions in a vertical column) for each trauma you would like to acknowledge. Then briefly answer each of the questions—just jot down your answers.

You don't need to list everything—just what you think is important from any time in your past. Also, try not to go into much detail. Because of ways you may have learned to handle trauma in the past, you may believe that "going deep" is necessary. In this exercise, I suggest you *don't* go deep into traumatic memories. It could distract you from the exercise and lure you away from present time, triggering you unnecessarily and derailing your progress on the exercise.

The purpose is to recall, in a simple way, why you might have CPTSD without minimizing these experiences. Some of this information may provide insight; at the very least, it can help you feel confident that your trauma is not being ignored. When it's done, put your journal away in a safe place (you can even tear out the pages where you list past traumas so they can be hidden in an *extra*-safe place). Then take your attention off the past so you focus on present-day symptoms in the upcoming chapters. You can refer to your list or update it whenever you like.

The first few lines show an example so you can get the general idea of the format.

TRAUMATIZING EXPERIENCES

WHAT HAPPENED	HOW IT MAY HAVE AFFECTED ME AT THE TIME	HOW IT AFFECTS ME TODAY
My parents fought violently in front of me many times, since I can remember.	I was anxious. Stomach problems probably about this. Knew by the time I was 5 to lie to grandparents and teacher.	I'm a "fighter" in relationships. Go from calm to freaked out VERY fast when someone yells. Can't calm down easily. Still feel like I have to lie about what goes on at home.
Two-year situationship with James. He was never into me and told me this was just friends with benefits. I said fine, but was obsessed for three years.	Depression. Shame. Dropped out of classes for two semesters and smoked pot every day. Lost friends because I was acting so crazy. Knew I should stop seeing him but didn't.	Don't trust myself in relationships. Always pretend I don't like people when I do like them. I don't believe they like me. Roger said I was never "real" and left.
5th grade kids called me "fat" all the time. Didn't invite me to birthdays and hanging out.	I hated my body. Got "tough" to show people I didn't mind not being included. Really bad self-esteem. I think part of this (and getting left out) was because my clothes were dirty, shabby. Same outfit most days.	I still hate my body!!! So many problems with food. So much feeling lonely. I have subtle belief that other people all fit in with each other, but (for reasons I don't understand) I don't belong.

FOR YOUR JOURNAL
. . . .

- What did it feel like to acknowledge these traumas all in one place?

- Have you had the chance to tell the story of these traumatic experiences to an understanding person? If so, what was that like? Is it something you'd like to do more in the future?

- When you think about the factors that helped you to survive what happened and to build your life anyway, were there people, groups, or experiences that gave you confidence and/or a sense of safety?

- Are you ready to "rest" the story of the past for a bit while you shift your focus toward practical steps to heal your present-day symptoms?

If this or any exercise feels upsetting or heavy, or it makes you feel triggered, pause your work and take steps to calm your nervous system. You'll find a list of steps you can take to do this on pages 69–71.

I promise you: You really are capable of healing and making good changes in your life. Improving your relationships, your mental and physical health, and your overall level of happiness is going to get much, much easier, especially when you *learn to re-regulate*.

So how do people do that?

In the next chapter, I'll take you on a brief tour of some common CPTSD treatment methods, including some that can help you re-regulate and others that "skip over" the need to re-regulate. Perhaps you've tried some of them already. Thinking through what has worked and what has not worked for you in the past will help to guide you as you continue with this work.

CHAPTER 2

TRAUMA TREATMENTS OLD AND NEW—
AND HOW THIS APPROACH IS DIFFERENT

If you have ever sought professional help for trauma-related symptoms, you had every right to expect that the practitioner's expertise and the treatments you tried would help you feel better and support you in making lasting changes in your life.

But did they?

There are good and caring practitioners out there, and some treatments that many people find helpful. If you've had good results with any of these, then stay with them and keep reading.

The problem is, many of us with CPTSD have found little benefit or have not been helped at all by the industry-standard approaches to trauma healing that dominate the field—namely, talk therapy and medication. Evidence is wobbly that they are the most effective, or even effective at all, for CPTSD.

If you had a disappointing experience with these treatments, you may have thought it was "just you." But it may have had more to do with the fact that these methods didn't specifically help with dysregulation, and trying to work through trauma *while* you're dysregulated can make dysregulation even worse.

Also, there's little transparency around what healing modalities work and which individual practitioners get the best results.

We have few ways of knowing who *really* knows their stuff about trauma versus those who have merely gone to a workshop or two and now post on their therapist profiles that they treat trauma.

If you've been trying and failing to get help for problems connected to your own childhood trauma, it's definitely not just you! And it's especially important to read this chapter, because it might just explain *why* nothing you've tried so far has worked, and this can free you to pursue methods that might be a better fit for you.

Finding your best options can be tricky. If you search for answers (online, for example, or from your doctor) on how Childhood PTSD can be healed, you'll find constant repetition of the idea that you always need to see a mental-health professional, because (a) they have the answers and (b) it will help. It's a bit like the relationship of the old USDA food pyramid to nutrition: Anyone who reads on the subject knows the standards are wrong, out-of-date, and strangely resistant to the 21st-century research.

In my approach to healing, I encourage *you* to be the judge of what works for you. Seek advice and help from experts, but never unquestioningly—not from therapists or doctors, and not from me! Learn by trying what you think might work, and don't hesitate to drop treatments that don't.

In this chapter, I'll give you an overview of standard treatment modalities as well as some newer and alternative treatments (including brain-based and body-based methods) that some people have found helpful. And I'll tell you more about my method and why it's different.

WHY THE STANDARD TREATMENT MAY NOT BE THE BEST

Just because a treatment is frequently recommended doesn't mean it's effective.

The most common treatments by far are talk therapy and medication, or a combination of both. Most people with CPTSD have at least *tried* one or both of them. Let's start with **medication**.

A surprising percentage of people worldwide—one in seven Americans and one in six people in the UK—take medication for depression and anxiety, conditions that are especially common in people with trauma. If you seek help for these problems, it's highly likely you will be prescribed antidepressants and/or antianxiety medication.

With CPTSD, these medications can be somewhat helpful to calm certain acute symptoms, though in many cases they can delay recovery by dulling awareness, producing what many of us call "brain fog." If you have neurological dysregulation, medication can also inhibit the natural processes by which you would be able to return to a regulated state. The drugs are not specifically designed for re-regulation, and their effects don't match very well with our symptoms.

There can be serious side effects to these medications too, including thoughts of harming yourself or others, sexual difficulties, and a sense of numbness when trying to make decisions or connect with others—all significant for people trying to heal. Medications may provide a mood shift, but they don't offer a cure. Side effects and benefits stop as soon as medication is discontinued.

Traditional talk therapy (including cognitive behavioral therapy or CBT, which aims to help you notice and replace distorted or unhelpful ways of thinking and behaving) is *the* standard of our times for a wide range of problems, including depression, anxiety disorders, addictions, and severe mental illness. Many assume it will help people with trauma, but evidence for that is, at best, conflicting.

Other kinds of talk therapy that have been used for trauma include cognitive processing therapy, exposure therapy, and dialectical behavior therapy. These focus on aspects of trauma such as memories, sensitivity to triggers, and regulation of emotions. But do they work? "Traumatized people often have enormous difficulty telling other people what has happened to them," says Dr. van der Kolk. "Their bodies reexperience terror, rage, and helplessness, as well as the impulse to fight or flee, but these feelings are almost impossible to articulate."[1]

Used separately or together, talk therapy and medication are the default treatments for people who are suffering emotionally, and many people say they have found them helpful. But in a 2022 study published by the British Medical Association, researchers from the FDA's Center for Drug Evaluation and Research, Johns Hopkins, and the Cleveland Clinic found that antidepressant drugs don't work for at least 85 percent of people who take them.[2] All in all, they are just 2 percent more effective than a placebo[3]—and that's for depression. For healing the effects of trauma from childhood, there is very little evidence that they work at all.

Still, talk therapy and medication absorb almost all public resources available for treating adults with trauma. Almost nothing outside of these conventional methods is covered by private insurance or national health programs, even though there are more effective treatments available and even though there is a risk that conventional treatments can make CPTSD symptoms worse.

With so many people suffering (and the cost of CPTSD symptoms so high), why is there so little curiosity about better approaches to treatment? Why isn't there more research and more inclusion of methods that *do* work in standard treatment plans, covered by insurance—if for no other reason than that effective treatment can prevent costly chronic illness?

This is beginning to change, but most adults treated for trauma-related symptoms will go round and round the merry-go-round of the old system—therapy, medication, new therapist, new medication, and so on—and never really improve. After a while, when hope fades, traumatized people tend to blame themselves, believing there must be something extra wrong with them.

To be effective, trauma treatments must address the core trauma injury (which is at least partly neurological) and not just the downstream symptoms like depression and anxiety. For sustained healing that helps you progressively build a happy life, you'll need to heal the nervous-system injury that leaves you prone to dysregulation. Dysregulation makes everything else about life—including your work to heal yourself—difficult.

Remember, Childhood PTSD is, at its foundation, *neurological*. It develops in relation to brain changes caused by abuse, neglect, and other intensely stressful conditions in childhood. This results in intermittent states of emotional, cognitive, and physiological dysregulation that can render you unable to benefit from any therapy, no matter how helpful it's been to nontraumatized people who have an easier time staying neurologically regulated.

When you're dysregulated, it can be hard to pay attention, remember, communicate, and learn. You may feel clumsy, panicked, lost, or (literally) numb. In a dysregulated state, it's very easy to miss danger signals, to emotionally overreact, or to make serious, life-altering errors of judgment. It can be dangerous to drive. So this just might explain why your experiences in therapy have felt so upsetting and pointless.

If therapy left you dysregulated and unable to make progress, it's likely that medication was recommended, which (we now know) may have made it even harder to regain a regulated state so you could work on making positive changes. If you are prone to dysregulation, it might explain why medication and talk therapy couldn't touch your Childhood PTSD symptoms.

If therapists or doctors don't *themselves* tend to get dysregulated under stress, it must seem like these conventional approaches to treatment ought to be effective. But there is no clear evidence that they are a good line of treatment.

In fact, for people who tend to get dysregulated, talking about troubling memories (as is common in therapy) can make things worse; we get *more* upset and less able to think, analyze, or remember what was said. When I was most desperate for help and going to therapy three times a week, I'd arrive at sessions focused and hopeful, and leave 50 minutes later so distraught and dysregulated I couldn't feel my hands. I could barely turn the doorknob to walk out of the office. I'd have to sit in my car for 45 minutes, crying and trying to calm down enough to drive. When I talked to my therapist about this, she said I was "processing a lot of stuff," that I had to "grieve before I could heal," and that it was "going to take a long time."

I didn't know better than to accept this advice back then; she was the expert, and I was desperate. But as you may have already noticed, I no longer unconditionally accept professional opinions, only because in the past, the help I received was not always helpful—and sometimes harmful. Thousands of people tell me their experiences in therapy have been complicated like this too.

NEWER AND ALTERNATIVE TREATMENTS FOR TRAUMA

I believe it's essential for traumatized people to address dysregulation, which by necessity involves a new approach to treatment. One sign that your treatment does work is that you are able to process thoughts and emotions (including grief) more efficiently than before, you are able to remember and manage treatment strategies and goals from day to day, and you begin to feel better and more hopeful quite early in the process. These are benefits of mastering re-regulation.

Each person with CPTSD is different, and we respond to different things. When you become sovereign over your healing, you are free to reject treatments that you don't find helpful and to try those that seem like they could be a fit for you. Keep an open mind! Many, many medical and mental-health professionals are actively engaged with new research and revising standard approaches to care.

Below is a list of treatments where there is *some* evidence of effectiveness.

Brain and Nervous-System-Focused Therapies

Developed by Francine Shapiro, *eye movement desensitization and reprocessing* (EMDR) is a powerful technique, endorsed by the U.S. Department of Veterans Affairs, that helps to integrate the traumatic memories typical of trauma. In PTSD, the activation of certain memories produces an intense psychological and physiological distress (nightmares, pounding heart, outbursts of rage) as though the event is happening in this very moment. These reactions occur again and again and don't tend to diminish over time.

EMDR involves the use of controlled, side-to-side eye movements, vibrating handheld paddles, or other tools that alternately stimulate the left and right brain. The practitioner helps you to visit traumatic memories and then "reprocess" them so they become more like a normal memory—remembered, but not so intensely charged. Strictly speaking, you don't have to talk during EMDR, which can be helpful for those of us who tend to dysregulate when talking about what happened. The effects are long-lasting; occasionally those who have benefited from it will opt to come back for EMDR sessions months or years later.

EMDR is one modality that worked powerfully to help me stop intrusive thoughts about some recent traumas in my adult life—but only with a practitioner who did not require me to talk much about the trauma.

Polyvagal therapy is an approach pioneered by Stephen Porges that focuses on the three interconnected branches of the autonomic nervous system and their role in regulating your response to stress and trauma. Polyvagal therapy aims to balance the ventral-vagal state (associated with a sense of calm, safety, connection, and emotional well-being); the sympathetic state (associated with your fight-or-flight response); and the dorsal-vagal state, which can lead to a spaced-out or "freeze" response when you feel threatened. Several devices are available that electrically stimulate the polyvagal nerve, which can help to bring it out of a dysregulated state.

Neurofeedback, developed in the 1950s by Joe Kamiya and Barry Sterman, is another treatment that shows some promise for CPTSD. The practitioner attaches electrodes to your face and scalp to measure brain activity when you're in a relaxed state versus in a stress response. You then receive some kind of stimulus—such as listening to sounds or watching a video—that changes with your brain states. When I tried it, I watched a travel video on a screen that went dark whenever my brain was unfocused or stressed; it brightened when I calmed my mind. We're barely conscious of what we're doing, but apparently our brains can learn from this form of biofeedback to reach a relaxed, alert state and stay there more of the time. It can take dozens of sessions to get lasting results, which can be a drawback if you don't have good health insurance. But many have found it helpful.

Brainspotting, developed by David Grand, involves moving your eyes to locate the "brainspot" or eye position that is associated with a traumatic memory or trauma response. It's somewhat similar to EMDR. The thought is that once you find the spot (usually with the help of a therapist), your brain can resume processing a trauma that got "stuck." People who have found brainspotting helpful say it works relatively quickly and does not require that you talk about the memory while you use the technique, which can be big plus for those of us who tend to get dysregulated when we talk about trauma.

Psychedelics offer promise as treatment for trauma. At the time of this writing, clinical trials are underway and approvals may be imminent. MDMA, psilocybin, and ketamine, for example, are being tested not as treatments only for CPTSD but for depression, anxiety, and addiction. Early results show that with trained practitioners, psychedelic therapy could be a good way to break through trauma that's stuck.

Tapping, also called Emotional Freedom Techniques (EFT), is a method that a lot of people swear by. It involves actually tapping your face, head, torso, and hands along the body's meridians (a concept originating in Chinese medicine) to calm anxiety and harsh emotions. There are terrific videos on YouTube that show you how to do it, tapping with your fingertips along acupressure points or meridians. Some say the benefits are just a placebo effect, but others use it daily to manage triggers and reactions.

Body-Based Therapies

Some experts think that trauma is "stored" in the body, so movement and raised awareness of your body can help to release it. Peter Levine developed one prominent therapy of this type: *Somatic Experiencing*, in which a practitioner guides you to notice how emotions and memories are connected to sensations in the body and then to release them.

Some other body-based treatments for trauma include activities you may already be doing, including martial arts (for example, qigong and tai chi), dance, and yoga, which have each been used for thousands of years. These activities involve movement, with awareness of the right and left sides of the body; they're often performed in a group and in response to a voice calling out directions. All of these factors are re-regulating, and I suspect that people in past generations used them—as well as marching in formation, call-and-response songs, and chanting—as means of calming and focusing the nervous systems too.

In recent years, yoga professionals have developed yoga styles specifically designed for treating trauma. This means there is sensitivity around feelings and memories that could be triggered by certain poses, as well as an emphasis on being conscious and gentle with whatever may be triggered.

The Wim Hof Method includes special deep-breathing exercises and cold exposure (cold showers or ice baths) as a means to "reset" the nervous system, stimulate the release of serotonin and dopamine, and lift your mood; it's free, easy to practice at home, and very popular.

It's now clinically proven that *vigorous exercise* is perhaps the most effective treatment for depression, anxiety, brain fog, and overall stress; it's therefore an essential part of trauma treatment. "Vigorous" means any form of movement that elevates your heart rate, especially if you break a sweat; perform it for 45 minutes if you're physically able.

Healthy eating is also a factor in trauma healing. A diet that limits sugar, flour, and other processed food or "fast" carbs can help your mind stay focused and your nervous system regulated, and it can keep your mood more upbeat and steady too. The inclusion of protein in each meal is helpful. Some people find that coffee can help with staying neurologically regulated; others have noticed that caffeine totally throws them off.

Internal Family Systems Therapy

Internal Family Systems, also known as IFS, or Parts Therapy, is a form of psychotherapy developed in the 1980s by Richard Schwartz. It is based on the idea that a person has "parts" or sub-personalities that interact to influence thinking and behavior—sometimes in conflict with each other—and function to protect the person from trauma and pain. IFS therapy aims to help a person understand and integrate these parts, as a means to heal trauma.

There are many other trauma therapies available, but answers about their effectiveness are limited. They include hypnosis, vagus nerve stimulation, stellate ganglion blocks, Lifespan Integration therapy, acceptance and commitment therapy, and Havening techniques. More treatments are being tried and tested all the time. If you encounter a method I haven't covered here, I encourage you to investigate if it might be helpful to you.

FOR YOUR JOURNAL

• • • • • • •

- What healing methods have you tried?
- What has helped so far? What changed? Did the changes last over time?
- What has *not* worked for you? Why?
- Are you ready to become sovereign over your own healing? What would you do differently once you truly took charge?

MY APPROACH TO HEALING AND WHY IT'S DIFFERENT

In my method of healing, you won't be focusing specifically on the trauma that happened to you, though it may be important to name those wounds, as you did at the end of Chapter 1.

Nor will you be focused specifically on your body or the notion that trauma is trapped there, though physical exercise is important for healing—and you may find that your physical health improves as your overall trauma healing progresses.

In my method, the work centers on healing these three areas, which I call "the three-legged stool":

1. DYSREGULATION (nervous system and emotional)

2. DISCONNECTION from others (e.g., feeling different, left out, or isolated; having difficulty forming good friendships)

3. SELF-DEFEATING BEHAVIORS (e.g., addictions, attraction to unavailable people, emotional outbursts, money problems)

Each of these areas—dysregulation, disconnection, and self-defeating behaviors—flow into each other and influence each other in good ways and bad. When you heal in one area, the other areas get a boost for healing as well. Likewise, when you're having setbacks in one area, the other areas are more vulnerable to setbacks too.

My method is designed to help you change your life in ways that matter, quickly. You'll focus on:

*   ESTABLISHING A CALM AWARENESS THROUGH THE DAILY PRACTICE techniques so you have a means to process thoughts and emotions and find rest, comfort, and insight that sustain you through the work of healing

*   REDUCING HOW MUCH YOU TALK ABOUT TRAUMA, writing about it instead

*   OWNING YOUR HEALING and not relying on another person to make healing happen for you

- KEEPING THE FOCUS ON YOUR OWN TRAUMA-DRIVEN THINKING, BELIEFS, AND ACTIONS rather than on what others do or have done

- PRIORITIZING PRESENT-TIME PROBLEMS (which you can change) rather than events of the past

- STEPPING UP IN LIFE, aiming not only to feel better or solve problems, but to become your full and real self and bring your unique gifts into the world

WHY DAILY WRITING IS CRITICAL TO THIS METHOD OF HEALING

While processing traumatic experiences is necessary, processing it by *talking* about it can trigger dysregulation. Talking activates the amygdala, which is the part of your brain that's heavily involved in processing emotions, especially the feeling of being under threat. This prompts your body to release stress hormones, and if you're talking a *lot* about what happened, it can overwhelm you with a state called "emotional arousal," similar to the state you'd be in if the trauma were actually happening in present time.

Talking about trauma can also activate your hypothalamic-pituitary-adrenal (HPA) axis. This refers to the interaction between the hypothalamus, pituitary, and adrenal glands that work together when you're going through actual trauma and that help you protect yourself and get out of danger. Activating the HPA axis again and again just by talking about the past can have negative effects on your physical health and on your psychological health. When I told you that I used to have to cry in my car for 45 minutes after therapy visits, this is what was going on.

Talking about your trauma can also produce wild swings in the functioning of your prefrontal cortex; your ability to reason and make decisions gets suppressed, and your emotions go through the roof. It can also impact neurotransmitter levels in your brain, including dopamine and serotonin, which go *way* up and then *way* down—diminishing your sense of being okay and safe and able to face your life.

So, talking about trauma can make it worse, but we *need* a way to process these emotions and the memories of what happened. "Processing" means your brain and nervous system can review the memory, interpret it, and then file it appropriately as a memory, not "a terrifying thing that's happening right now."

Unprocessed thoughts and emotions are precisely what accumulate in a traumatized mind—we're not able to fully process them under stress. It's why focus is hard. It's why emotions are too large and/or absent at the weirdest times. And it's why you go around feeling so totally overwhelmed by simple things like speaking up in class, saying no to someone asking you for money, or just calming down after a loud noise. There's too much bouncing around in your awareness. Your thinking gets noisy with unprocessed thoughts and emotions.

So, this is where writing comes in and saves the day.

The Therapeutic Value of Writing

Writing is a way you *can* process emotions without all the triggers involved in speaking about the trauma. My experience is, I can write it and read it to someone and stay regulated; if I just speak it, I get dysregulated. No matter how much I know about trauma and dysregulation, that's how my brain works.

Research studies have shown that writing about trauma can be powerfully therapeutic. Among the most significant is the work of Dr. James W. Pennebaker at the University of Texas, Austin, who developed a technique he calls "expressive writing." It's a structured method to reduce symptoms of depression and anxiety, and it has been shown to work effectively against trauma as well.

In Pennebaker's technique, you write for 15 to 30 minutes about the most traumatic experience you can remember and then repeat the exercise four days in a row. More than 200 peer-reviewed studies have validated the positive effects of expressive writing. It has helped to reduce depression and anxiety, improve well-being, and measurably improve physical health. And these benefits are not just at the time of writing—they last long term. This an astonishing outcome from such a simple intervention.

There are downsides noted as well. Namely, people who use this technique often feel emotionally overwhelmed as they do the work. In my opinion, so much focus on the *most* traumatic experience you can remember could be too much for people with CPTSD, possibly triggering worse emotional and neurological states.

In the Daily Practice, we adjust for these possibilities. We don't go straight for the worst memory. As you'll learn in the next chapter, you write only the distressing thoughts that are on your mind at the time of writing. If you do it every day, twice a day, your worst memories are bound to arise eventually, so you will have the chance to process them. But the organic pacing (writing things as they pop up in your mind) and *daily* habit of the writing is more likely to be sustainable and to bring more relief than overwhelm.

Second, we follow the writing in the Daily Practice immediately with restful meditation. I've observed during my 30 years of teaching the techniques that people who do *only* the writing portion of the exercise enjoy the technique for a week or two but soon become overwhelmed or exhausted. They give up. Those who do the meditation are more likely to find the Daily Practice comforting and refreshing, day after day. The meditation brings rest, re-regulation, and deeper healing after every single writing session, and the benefits of regular meditation in any context are well documented.

I love that writing is something any of us can practice anytime, anywhere, alone or in groups, for free. We don't have to wait for something to come heal us. We heal and re-regulate ourselves.

But the Daily Practice has even more to offer. The only way for you to know what it does for you is to give it a try.

Are you ready? Let's begin!

CHAPTER 3

THE DAILY PRACTICE

The problem with healing trauma is that its *symptoms* make it so hard to focus or get things done that doing the work of healing can feel impossible.

Thank goodness there is the Daily Practice. This is the twin set of techniques that lifted me out of depression in 1994 and that I've continued to use for three decades now. The techniques are so simple and comforting that anyone can use them, even on the hardest days.

The first technique is a specific form of writing used to *face and release* fearful and resentful thoughts, followed immediately by the second technique, which is a simple form of restful meditation. They are practiced together—writing followed by meditation—twice a day.

Rachel, the woman who taught these to me, learned them from a woman she met in a meeting of Alcoholics Anonymous (she called them "the Daily Steps"). And she showed the techniques to her when she mentioned that though she was sober, she was miserable. As soon as she tried these Steps, she experienced relief, and 36 years later, she continues to practice twice a day and to teach them to others. (In the Appendix of this book, you'll find detailed FAQs about the use of the techniques, including the history of the Daily Steps and why I adapted them for non–12 Step use as "the Daily Practice" when I created Crappy Childhood Fairy.)

The Daily Practice was the very first thing that ever *really* helped me. I was willing to try it because I was desperate to feel better. When I wrote and meditated for the first time, I experienced relief, and my head cleared. Within two weeks my powers of perception and my ability to focus came back stronger than they'd ever been. In time, I was able to solve my problems and move in a positive direction, becoming less afraid and more myself.

This is what healing is: to recognize your symptoms when they're happening and to know what to do about them in the moment, wherever you happen to be. This is the foundation of how we master re-regulation.

Every kind of person can do this, even if they don't have CPTSD. My students have included men and women, small children, teenagers, and people in their 80s and 90s. They've included artists, engineers, clergy, entrepreneurs, medical and mental-health professionals, women in labor, and people in hospice care, in prison, or just going through a temporary crisis.

The techniques are easy to learn and can help you feel better right away. You can begin anytime, whether you have access to professional help or not. You can do this work alone or with friends, on a bus or in a room where other people are making noise, in person, or on Zoom. All you need is some paper and a pen or pencil.

The best way to find out what the Daily Practice is like is to begin, so let's get started with the first technique.

BEGIN BY WRITING YOUR FEARS AND RESENTMENTS

In this exercise, you'll use the scratch pad I suggested in the Introduction that you keep with you, along with a pen or pencil. You'll be following a specific format to name the fearful and resentful thoughts that are troubling your mind when you sit down to write. These negative and trauma-driven thoughts are like the "substance" of Childhood PTSD, which, left untreated, can drive negative states of mind and trauma-driven behaviors. So here, you are getting free of them.

The thoughts might be about the past, present, or future, but you aren't going searching for problems that are not already on your mind. You are clearing your mind of its current worries.

You'll be categorizing those negative thoughts into two "buckets": (1) fears and (2) resentments. There are many other negative emotions, but in this part of the exercise, we keep things simple, calling all negative emotions and thoughts either "fear" (the anxious kind of thought) or "resentment" (the angry kind of thought).

If you follow these instructions, the process can help you release pent-up emotions and worries (for a while at least) and make room for new ideas and inspiration to arise. Doing the Daily Practice consistently can help you feel calmer and more alert, and it can comfort you when you're feeling grief, panic, or overwhelm.

Here's how to do it:

- Gather your scratch pad (or any kind of paper) and a pen or pencil. Sit down to write for 5 or 10 minutes. You can write longer than that if you like.

- Begin by writing the words "I have fear" and then complete the sentence with whatever comes to mind— something you're actually feeling anxious about. For example, "I have fear this won't work."

- Then write some more. For example: "I have fear I'm unfixable. Fear Jim is waiting for me outside and I'll be late."

- Your fears don't have to *sound* like fears. They are anything that worries your mind about the past, present, or future. They may be true or they may not. You don't have to know, either way. They can be trivial or important. For example: "I have fear my shirt needs ironing. I have fear this lump in my breast is cancer." All fears, big and small, clutter your mind in the same way. If a thought is bothering you, just put it on paper.

- Try to let the words flow from your pencil or pen without analysis, and try not to dig for more than comes to you.

- Don't look for patterns (though you may notice patterns sometimes).

- Don't worry that naming these thoughts will make them "manifest." Since they are bothering your mind, we can assume they already manifested, and you're doing the Daily Practice to be free of them.

- Don't try to focus on a specific topic or make the exercise deliver a specific feeling or answer to you (though they may come on their own sometimes). Just name the fearful thoughts—worries and memories—that are going through your mind at the time you are writing and see what happens.

- Don't worry about grammar or spelling; only you will see this. This is your chance to dump raw thoughts that are fearful and resentful out of your mind and onto paper.

- Don't modify the format.

As you're writing, don't take the word *fear* too literally. The kind of fear we're after is not (for example) a phobia, like a fear of snakes. It's more like a worry: "Fear I said too much at lunch today. Fear I was embarrassed. Fear I didn't leave a big-enough tip," and so on. You don't need to dig or try to write everything in your life all at once (if you continue using the Daily Practice twice a day, you'll eventually get to all of it).

You don't need to write the fears and resentments in any particular order. Just write what comes into your mind. It might be an old memory that comes to you, followed by something that has just happened. It could be some anxiety about the future. These are thoughts that are already on your mind—things you're worried about (or even freaking out about).

As you're writing, you'll also want to write resentments— things that make you feel angry (resentment at others) or guilty or ashamed (resentment at yourself). Anger is not a problem; it's natural and necessary sometimes, and there's no need to push it down or eradicate it. You can think of resentment as anger that's *festering*—a thought that loops around in your mind long after the anger is serving you. But even if you feel your resentful feelings are justified or just normal anger, write them down. Better to include too much than not enough.

When you notice a resentment, it probably *feels* something like this: "I'm sick and tired of my wife; here she goes, getting upset again."

When you do the Daily Practice, though, you write this resentment in a special way that goes like this: "I'm resentful at my wife because I have fear she's upset again."

In this case, "my wife" is the *target*, and "she's upset again" is the *reason*.

So, that's the format for all resentments: *I'm resentful at* (target) *because I have fear* (reason).

You're probably wondering why we insert "because I have fear." First, it leaves a little room for open-mindedness about whether what we perceive is actually true (sometimes it is, sometimes it isn't). Even if we *know* for a fact that your wife is upset again—she said so, and she's standing in the doorway crying—we say, "I have fear she's upset again" for good measure.

The second reason is, resentment grows when anger is tangled with fear. So if you had no fear (which would never happen for long, but let's just say hypothetically you had no fear), your anger would pass without turning into resentment.

In other words, you're resentful *because* you have fear. So we write, "I'm resentful at my wife *because I have fear* she's upset again."

There's often a cluster of fears tangled up in each resentment, so it can help to linger a moment when you're writing a resentment to see if there is more to add: "I'm resentful at my wife because I have fear she's upset again. Fear she always gets upset when my parents are in town. Fear she's rude to them, and fear now Mom is tense and fear I'll end up losing my temper."

(Notice that after the first time you write "I have fear," you can write just "fear" as shorthand for "I have fear.")

When you're resentful, it's important to have a target. It could be one of several things:

- a person

- a group of people (such as "the neighbors" or "the restaurant owners")

- a category of people (criminals, "lousy drivers," or people who follow a particular religion, for example)

- an organization ("the IRS")

- a country

- God (because you don't like the human condition, the weather, or immutable characteristics in your body, for example)

- yourself (because you regret what you said or did, for example)

Your target is always a person or group (or God), not a feeling or event. We might resent nonhuman phenomena (e.g., "deadlines" or "the sexual revolution"), but they can't function as targets, because the blame rests *beyond* them—with the people who made them happen.

Here's another example: Let's say you feel resentful at your child's teachers because they allowed kids to be bullies. That is the structure of your thought, but if you're writing it as part of your Daily Practice, you'll write it like this:

"I'm resentful at the teachers *because I have fear* they allowed kids to be bullies."

I've italicized the phrase "because I have fear" to make sure you see it there. This is the piece that people new to these techniques tend to forget, but it is crucial if you are to get relief from your resentment.

If you're just listing a bunch of resentments (and not acknowledging the role of fear in making them so troubling), you're just ranting. Research confirms that ranting is not cathartic or reliev-ing; in fact, it makes resentment worse. So always, always include "because I have fear" when you name your resentments, and consider pausing to see if there are other fears amplifying your resentment as well.

Everyone has fears, and the ones that drive resentment often have to do with fairness, survival, and belonging. The fears and resentments don't have to be true, and they don't have to be import-ant. They are written as a stream of consciousness. Just let them out. Call every single one of them either a fear or a resentment.

Don't go into a big narrative; *this is not a journal.* We're not trying to document or remember what happened; nor do we need to analyze it. We're just dumping every little thought onto paper with the words "I have fear" before it. Or, if it's a resent-ment, "I am resentful at (target) because I have fear . . . (the rea-son)," and then back into the fears, in whatever order you become aware of them.

You're not in denial. You're not stuffing your feelings down or ignoring them. You're getting them off your mind and onto paper so that crabby tyrant inside your head can have a little vacation for a few hours and you can be calm, alert, and gentle inside. When you're in this state, good things often happen.

Some Ways You Might Get Stuck When You Write

YOU MAY FEEL A NEED TO BE GOAL ORIENTED IN THE DAILY PRACTICE. The goal is simply to release mental clutter (fear and resentment), for the same reason you clear your windshield when it's covered with wet leaves. You don't need to pick up each wet leaf, to study it, press it in a book, and label it. No, you just fling the leaves into the street and drive the car! More leaves may accumulate on your windshield later, just as new fears and resentments (and many of the old ones) will return to your mind soon enough. But the time you spend with a spacious mind gives you a chance to get regulated and calm and to access parts of your mind that are not normally available to you. In time these "reprieves" produce a cumulative healing effect, reducing trauma symptoms and strengthening the skills you need to solve problems and lead a happy life.

YOU MIGHT WORRY THAT RELEASING YOUR FEARS AND RESENTMENTS WILL LEAVE YOU DEFENSELESS, thinking, "I need my fear or I'll forget to get a mammogram!" But your anxious thinking is not the best way to keep track of appointments (a calendar is). Or you might feel that your resentments are the only thing protecting you from others walking all over you. But living life angry and defensive is not a good substitute for having boundaries.

With the Daily Practice, you'll find ways to safely release fear and resentment so that you can be both lighthearted *and* a high-functioning person.

SOME PEOPLE WORRY THAT SAYING, "I'M RESENTFUL AT SO-AND-SO BECAUSE I HAVE FEAR THEY HURT ME" IS GASLIGHTING THEMSELVES, since the hurt really happened. Again, don't worry whether your fears and resentments are real or unreal, justified or not. You are just writing thoughts that bother you and naming and acknowledging the fears and resentments at play.

YOU MIGHT WORRY THAT ACKNOWLEDGING THESE DARK FEELINGS WILL MAKE THEM WORSE. Remember, though, you are not *digging up* thoughts and feelings that you didn't already have; you are just naming the thoughts and feelings that are presently intruding on your mind. Naming them and writing them down—and especially releasing them or asking for them to be removed—is how you get freedom from them. You'll have less ruminating and more fresh thinking about your here-and-now reality.

Relax and See Where the Daily Practice Takes You

Even though we don't *look* for patterns in this exercise, you may see patterns and gain better perspective and insight. It will become easier to see what's actually a problem and what's not a problem after all. You'll become aware when you're overreacting to something, or when a problem needs your attention. The hectic thoughts that tend to turn in your mind will settle down for a while.

The purpose of this very specific writing exercise is to release these fears and resentments. Where do they go? Sometimes you'll begin the exercise with a head full of worries and forget most of them by the time you're done. Some of the worries will come into sharp focus, prompting you to take action.

Trust the process and assume your mind knows what to forget and what to remember. I often think of the writing as WD-40, the solvent that melts rust and leaves metal parts clean and useful. Your Daily Practice is helping your mind organize itself, forgetting some things and prioritizing others. The more your mind is free of cluttered thinking, the more space there is for inspiration, intuition, and insight.

Write for as long as needed to feel some rest and relief, if you can. On busy days you may only have time to write, "I have fear I don't have time to write." That's okay. On hard days there may be tears while you write, and it goes on for an hour. This is okay too. On most days, you'll probably find that 5 to 15 minutes is enough to feel complete. Then it's time to sign off.

Signing Off

This is the point of all the writing. The sign-off is a written prayer in which you ask for your fears and resentments to be removed. If you prefer a secular sign-off, you can "release" them instead (see examples on the next page).

No matter what, don't skip the sign-off! Without it, you're just listing a lot of problems. It can be helpful to write with the ending in mind: Write your fears and resentment as a prayer or as an admission of what it is that's burdening you, all as preparation for the moment when you release these fears and resentments or ask for them to be removed.

I suggest you choose one of two formats to use while you're getting the hang of the technique:

SPIRITUAL SIGN-OFF: "I am now ready, and I humbly ask that you, God, remove these fears and resentments. I pray to know your will for me today and to have the power to carry it out."

SECULAR SIGN-OFF: "I am now ready and hereby release these fears and resentments so that I can have a clearer vision of what I should do today, and so I'll have the focus, the energy, and the inner calm to do that to the best of my ability."

Then sign your name: "Love, Anna."

In the first version (the one I've always used), you might recognize the language of the 12 Steps, reflecting the origins of these techniques in the Daily Steps that I learned when I first got started.

When you've used the Daily Practice consistently for a week, you'll know the gist of it and can then customize your sign-off if you wish. I recommend that you honor the general spirit of the words that contain these four intentions:

1. I am ready now

2. I want to be free of these fears and resentments

3. I need to know where my thoughts and efforts should be directed

4. I seek the inner power to act on this knowledge

Now that your writing is done, it's a good time to destroy what you wrote! Remember, it's not a journal. You don't need to reread the pages or return to them in the future. (An exception is if you are working with a buddy or mentor and you intend to read to them what you wrote that day. I'll talk about buddies in the Appendix.)

The goal of the writing is to release your fears and resentments. You want the pages to be a safe place for you to tell the truth about thoughts in your mind, including the ugliest, most embarrassing thoughts that you have about your life and the people you know. So shred or burn your writing when you're done. Destroying the pages is not necessary to release the fears and resentments (that's already been accomplished through the sign-off). You destroy the pages to maintain your privacy and protect other people from being hurt.

Here's what an example of what fears and resentments, with a sign-off, might look like:

> I have fear I didn't get enough sleep. Fear lack of sleep makes my ADHD worse. Fear I'm always tired. Fear therefore I don't exercise. Fear now I look awful in my good jeans. Fear I won't get to sleep on time tonight. I'm resentful at L. because I have fear he snores and keeps me awake. Fear he won't do anything about the snoring because (fear) he doesn't care about me. Fear I'm always with people who don't care about me. Fear I always feel I have to hide my anger or L. will freak out and leave. Fear if he leaves I can't afford this place. Fear it's a matter of time before he leaves and (fear) I should leave him first.

> SPIRITUAL SIGN-OFF: I am now ready and humbly ask that you, God, remove these fears and resentments. I pray to know your will for me today, and to have the power to carry it out. Love, Jane

> Or . . .

> SECULAR SIGN-OFF: I am now ready and hereby release these fears and resentments. I seek now a clear vision of what I am to do today, and the energy, focus, and inner calm I need to do it well. Love, Jane

AFTER WRITING, REST YOUR MIND WITH MEDITATION

After you're done writing, it's time to sit down and take a rest in meditation for 20 minutes. When I first learned the Daily Practice, my friend suggested I learn Transcendental Meditation, and I found it both comforting and forgiving enough that I could keep to the recommended schedule of 20 minutes, twice a day.

You may be an established meditator in a different method, in which case using your usual style of meditation will be the easiest for you (and easy is what we want).

If you don't have an established meditation practice, you can try my Super Simple Meditation technique; that will tide you over for as long as you like. If you find the writing and meditating to be helpful and you plan to continue, you may want to find a teacher and learn meditation formally; I have observed in my students that it is generally very helpful.

HOW TO MEDITATE THE SUPER SIMPLE WAY

While some meditation techniques focus on the breath, emptying the mind, or noticing your thoughts, the goal of Super Simple Meditation is simply to rest. The work of this practice is done while you write, and it's followed by restful meditation—a time for your brain and nervous system to rest and re-regulate, helping you to feel alert and refreshed afterward. If you're lucky, fresh thoughts and inspiration might come to you. Meditation will keep working no matter how it feels, but on most days, it won't be very eventful.

- Prepare a spot where you can sit comfortably for 20 minutes, undisturbed and safe, while you close your eyes.

- Sit in a dignified way, and avoid letting the back of your head rest on anything. It's okay to put your feet up, wrap yourself in a blanket, or otherwise make yourself comfortable.

- Set a timer, if you have one, so you don't have to keep looking at the time.

- To help you keep your focus on resting (instead of thinking), you may want to use a mantra. This is a sound that has no meaning—or it's a word that means something to you but that is neutral and calming to repeat to yourself, such as "Okay," or "This." I don't recommend using words that sound like goals or commands (like "Love one another" or "You can do it!"), since the goal is to just let go and relax and let the Daily Practice do its work.

- If you can't sit for 20 minutes, do what you can, but keep in mind that you'll get best results with 20 minutes of meditation, twice a day.

- If you forget to focus on the mantra and begin thinking, no problem. Just gently return to the mantra as soon as you realize your mind was wandering.

- If distractions happen (e.g., a kid runs into the room, or somebody rings the doorbell and you have to answer it), just pause your meditation and go deal with whatever it is, but then sit down and finish the 20 minutes.

- If you fall asleep during your meditation, that's okay. Again, just return to the mantra until your 20 minutes have elapsed.

- If there is noise around you, that's okay too. It's good to learn how to meditate with distractions.

- If you're *really* struggling with thinking, consider spending more time on your writing before your next meditation. Writing helps calm that mental chatter.

- If meditation brings up fearful thoughts, it's okay to keep it short for now.

- If you have a preferred form of meditation, use that one. But if you're not enjoying it, give my style of meditation a try. Sometimes it ends up getting better results because it's easier to stay with it long term.

- Twice a day is recommended because it works best to re-regulate your mind. But if you miss a meditation, don't worry about it!

- It can be nice to meditate with others, either in the same room or (if your meditation pals don't live near you) on a video conference call. I kid you not: It feels almost as if you're meditating in the same room.

- When your timer goes off, slowly open your eyes and give yourself a minute or two to come out of meditation. You're done!

When you first start using the Daily Practice, go ahead and take some time to just notice how you feel afterward. If you're like me, it's hard to sit still for 20 whole minutes. This is normal, and it doesn't mean you're doing it wrong.

Even if you felt restless, the meditation is providing rest, and you'll need it in order to continue doing the practice. Keep in mind that Childhood PTSD is a neurological injury, and the time you spend resting allows your nervous system to heal. This kind of quiet healing can't happen when you're busy doing things or watching TV. It's a profound change for your brain and body when you meditate for 20 minutes, two times a day.

On some days, you might get stuck without time to do your Daily Practice twice. It's okay if this happens. Do it once a day if that's all you can do. If you can't meditate for 20 minutes, do 10 minutes at first. But work on making room in your life for the important work of healing your nervous system with two 20-minute meditations.

Trust the process, knowing that if you put all your fears and resentments on paper, the items that actually need your attention will be there for you when you finish, and the rest may be safely allowed to vanish from memory.

Imagine you've taken a big pile of dirty clothes and rags to a laundry service. Half an hour later, you open your door and there on the doorstep is a tidy, square package of clean, folded clothes wrapped in blue paper. The rags are gone. This is something like the Daily Practice and how it cleans our thoughts and gives them back in better order.

DAILY PRACTICE TIPS

Here are some reminders to help you get started so that you can use the techniques each day, beginning today.

- Write first thing in the morning and again in the evening. You can write even more than that if you like, but make sure you write at least twice a day.

- You may be tempted to use the Daily Practice only occasionally, like an aspirin. It's meant for using regularly, like a toothbrush. So do it twice a day, whether you feel good or bad.

- Write as much as needed to feel better (at least a little better than when you started).

- Meditate immediately after writing, but don't meditate more than twice a day.

- There's no need to write well or look for insight. It's not a journal.

- Don't worry that releasing fears and resentments will leave you helpless or unable to set boundaries or act on problems. Trust that the release of troubling thoughts will only make you clearer and more effective.

- Be careful not to leave your writing where other people will see it and get their feelings hurt. Shred it, burn it, or write illegibly.

- When you're done writing, use one of the endings shown in the sample above, or write your own. Use your imagination to see those thoughts released (or removed) from your mind. Don't hold on to them, and don't dig up your whole life in a day. Just write and be rid of whatever thoughts are disturbing and dysregulating you right now. With less dysregulation, you'll have more clarity and strength to do good with your day and your life.

You'll find a comprehensive list of frequently asked questions about the Daily Practice in the Appendix.

YOUR FIRST DAILY PRACTICE

To get the most out of this book, I recommend you begin using the Daily Practice right away, before moving on to the next chapter. You can download a printable copy of the format—to use while you're learning and memorizing it—at **re-regulated.com.**

- Use your scratch pad, not your journal; you are taking out the trash of your mind and will not need the pages in the future.

- If you haven't done so already, take at least 10 minutes to write your fears and resentments, followed by the sign-off using the format given.

- Usually you will shred what you wrote right away, but for this first one, it's okay to keep it for a while until you've memorized how to do it and can write without checking the format. Feel free to reference this chapter to be sure you've got the format right.

- After you finish writing, sit down and close your eyes for a mini-meditation—at least five minutes. More is better. You can work your way up to 20 minutes within the next few days.

- After you're done meditating, shred or burn the paper you wrote on, and you're done.

FOR YOUR JOURNAL
• • • • • • • •

- After your first Daily Practice, notice any shifts in how you feel, and write them down.

- You may want to make a note of today's date so you'll always know when you first began.

Congratulations! You've done your first Daily Practice. You're now prepared and equipped to advance to the next chapter, where you'll begin work on the three-legged stool of trauma: dysregulation, disconnection, and self-defeating behaviors. This is where the real change begins!

CHAPTER 4

THE CORE SYMPTOM OF CHILDHOOD PTSD:
NEUROLOGICAL DYSREGULATION

Of all the things you'll learn in this book, the role of dysregulation in driving your trauma symptoms is the most important.

I've talked about it in each chapter so far, and now it's time to go deeper so you'll have the tools to recognize instantly when you're dysregulated neurologically or emotionally. I'll also teach you practical measures you can use to get re-regulated quickly and stay regulated more of the time.

In Chapter 5 I'll show you how to identify the feelings and experiences that *trigger* your dysregulation, both neurologically and emotionally, so you can either avoid them or learn to calm your reaction to them. And in Chapter 6, I'll teach you to recognize and calm emotional dysregulation (this is the kind other people easily notice).

If you're like me, you've known for a long time that something is "off" and different about you. Certain things in life that are easy for other people may feel nearly impossible for you. I'm the same way. Before I had much healing, my mental and emotional states were all over the place. I was often either agitated or groggy, stressed or wiped out. Sometimes I'd have good spells where I was energized and optimistic. But then, usually because of small things like feeling hurried or surprised by something, I'd get stressed and flustered again. When I felt hurt, my emotions would spike out of proportion with what was going on. As I got older—even though I'd been in therapy for years—the symptoms got worse, never better, and the ups and downs (especially the outbursts of anger) damaged my relationships. My inability to stay mentally focused held back my work and career prospects.

At the time, I thought I was just an unlikable person or that I was "cursed" with one failure after another. I couldn't see the pattern. No one ever told me I was showing signs of dysregulation that are typical in people who grew up with abuse and neglect or that I *could* learn to re-regulate. The reason they didn't tell me is because they didn't know.

Now we know, and finally the possibility of healing from past trauma is *wide* open to people like you and me.

It starts with learning to re-regulate. And to do that, we first need to learn when dysregulation is happening.

SIGNS OF DYSREGULATION

You will recognize some of these items from the general list of CPTSD symptoms from Chapter 1 that includes a few signs of dysregulation as well as other manifestations of trauma.

The list of questions below expands on this. As you read through it, take note of how many of these symptoms you've experienced and which ones affect you the most often.

- Do you tend to "space out" at odd times—in the middle of a conversation, for example, or when something stressful is happening?

- Do you often feel scattered, trying to do a lot of things at once and finishing nothing?

- Do you get clumsy at random times, tripping over things or dropping things?

- Do you ever notice you can't fully feel parts of your body—your hands, mouth, or face?

- When you are stressed, does your handwriting change?

- After a big emotional upset, do you sometimes feel nothing? Does your face go blank or your voice go flat when you feel upset?

- Do you have difficulty paying attention, even when it's important that you do?

- Do you have times when you struggle with short-term memory?

- When you're speaking, do you sometimes lose your words or have trouble completing sentences?

- Do you ever forget where you are? For example, when you're driving, do you ever get lost in a familiar place or struggle to remember familiar routes?

- Are you easily overwhelmed in certain environments (like crowds)?

- When you're trying to do something familiar (especially when you're hurrying or under pressure), do you sometimes get too flustered to function?

- When you're annoyed or angry with someone, do you ever feel a *huge* urgency to express your feelings, even when you know your emotional intensity is likely to cause things to get worse?

- Has your anger caused problems in your life—for example, ruining relationships, creating danger, or getting you in trouble with the law?

- Do you feel so overwhelmed when you set boundaries or stand up for yourself that you end up giving up or giving in?

FOR YOUR JOURNAL
• • • • • • • •

- How many of these signs of dysregulation have you experienced?
- Do some of these occur just occasionally? Are some of them more frequent?
- Has dysregulation ever put you in danger or damaged a relationship?

WHAT DOES *DYSREGULATED* ACTUALLY MEAN?

Dysregulation refers to a disruptive pattern of reactivity in the functioning of your nervous system. When it's triggered, it causes a change from the default, regulated state of your nervous system into a *dysregulated* state. In other words, things go "out of whack."

Imagine your regulated state as piano music that someone is playing beautifully. Dysregulation is like a cat that jumps onto the keys while the player keeps playing, overlaying the music with wrong notes that clang with random timing. The piano player can't focus and stops playing. Likewise, dysregulation is an intrusion of disruptive activity in your nervous system that impedes normal functioning.

Everyone gets dysregulated sometimes, and most of us eventually re-regulate without even realizing we're doing it. But people who were abused or neglected as children may spend more time in a dysregulated state and may have more difficulty re-regulating than other people.

Some signs of this are obvious, like an emotional outburst or a racing heart. But some signs are harder to notice, like the synchrony of your heartbeat with your breathing rate. When you're regulated, pulse and respiration flow together nicely, with your pulse rising slightly each time you inhale and slowing when you exhale (the variance in time between two heartbeats is called heart-rate variability, and it reflects cardiovascular health and nervous system states).

When you're dysregulated, your heart may beat irregularly and can go out of sync with your breathing. This (we now know) can increase the risk for disease and infection, all without *you* noticing anything is wrong.

For the most part, dysregulation is not something under your conscious control—though there are aspects of it that you can notice and consciously work to change.

Living dysregulated much of the time is a common state for those of us who endured trauma as children. You may never before have had a word for it nor had help for the problems it caused. If you're like many of us, you blamed yourself for having such a hard time with things that seem easy for everyone else. But now you know it's a neurological condition, and it's not your fault.

Part of neurological dysregulation is emotional dysregulation, which can happen to anyone at times but is extremely common in traumatized people. Emotional triggers are hard to control and can distort your perception of what's really happening. The emotions can be positive (like falling in love) or negative (like getting rejected), but when those emotions are dysregulated, they go out of proportion to the situation at hand—sometimes *way* out of proportion, and this is one aspect of CPTSD that can seriously harm relationships and is often involved in abusive behavior.

We'll cover emotional dysregulation more fully in Chapter 6. Here, let's explore *neurological* dysregulation, which is less visible to others (and therefore less well understood) but can be objectively seen and measured. An electroencephalogram (EEG) can measure brain waves, displaying them in a printed report as a series of wavy lines that represent brain activity in real time. When a nontraumatized person is responding to a stimulus of some kind (a noise, a touch, or someone speaking to them, for example) you'll see the lines flowing in a coordinated pattern, like a current of water that's traveling along smoothly. Brain scans on people traumatized as children show something quite different; the lines are somewhat out of sync, in a chaotic pattern, like water running over rocky rapids. Even when the stimulus isn't particularly scary or stimulating, you'll see irregular patterns. One reason is that trauma makes it harder for your brain to process information or to screen out irrelevant information. So there's a lot of superfluous brain activity (which is very much how neurological dysregulation *feels*).

Studies using MRI images of people who have past trauma and who are thinking stressful thoughts show a distinct change in brain activity too. For example, the left front cortex, where reasoning happens, becomes less active. And at the same time, the right front cortex, which processes emotions, lights up brightly. Ideally, when something makes you emotional, you'd want your ability to reason to also be active, helping you interpret what's going on and what to do. But with CPTSD, reasoning is suppressed and emotions are amplified (this matches how emotional dysregulation feels).

Some researchers believe that dysregulation may develop as a defensive response to unbearable stress when children's brains are developing. We may have become hyperalert to protect us from danger, or learned to dissociate to endure harms we couldn't escape. With our ability to respond to things around us varying between irrational vigilance and (seemingly) no vigilance at all, it's easy to see why traumatized people sometimes seem paranoid about risks and at other times make the same bad choices again and again. When you *say* you're never going to make a mistake again, and you *mean* you're never going to do it again . . . but then you look down and you're doing it again—that's a manifestation of dysregulation. People who don't get neurologically dysregulated find our behavior hard to understand.

With part of your brain not working properly, you are vulnerable and not fully yourself. You have trouble predicting the risks involved in impulsive decisions. Your perception is off, and you say things you don't really mean. Your thinking might seem true in the moment, but only because you're operating with half a brain!

WHAT DYSREGULATION FEELS LIKE

Those of us who had a rough childhood often go through life feeling (or knowing) that we are a little different from most people. Just being dysregulated is a problem that can make ordinary things in life ridiculously hard. Things like going on a date, spending time alone, expressing an opinion, or just buying a pair of shoes can knock our nervous system off-kilter, sending us into a haze of low energy and procrastination for hours . . . or days.

Being dysregulated is an awful feeling, but once in a while, we might "lean in" to dysregulation, because the way it shuts down our ability to function well is a kind of escape. When you can't function, at least you get to lie down!

But dysregulation has many aspects that you can't directly feel. Instead, you may only notice the "downstream" problems it causes in your physical health, cognitive functioning, and relationships. You may have intense back pain, struggle to keep track of time, or lose your temper at family members—promising yourself again and again to improve but never realizing that without learning to re-regulate, improvement can be nearly impossible.

A trigger happens, and your injured nervous system reacts. Stress hormones begin to flow, brain waves become irregular, and the same trauma-driven thinking and behaviors that have caused problems for you before are happening again, almost automatically.

First it's a feeling, almost like a migraine beginning or a drug running through your veins. The behaviors or feelings soon follow, including emotional outbursts and numbness, loss of focus, and trouble finishing thoughts. It can be impossible to complete tasks that you were in the middle of doing. And it can be hard to just pay attention; you're ruminating about something you remember while you're trying to pay attention to something right in front of you—like when you read the same paragraph over and over, but you keep spacing out and you can't remember either what you just read *or* what was distracting you.

When I'm dysregulated, I get clumsy and trip over my feet and drop things. I once broke four different dishes at different times in the same *day*. I can tell I'm dysregulated because, among other things, my handwriting changes and my nose feels numb.

You may have felt the symptoms of dysregulation and said you were "feeling discombobulated" or "out of your body," or you may have joked that you were having a "senior moment." You may have criticized yourself and felt ashamed (and, of course, feeling ashamed can trigger more dysregulation).

Dysregulation can also spread into your thinking and emotions. For a lot of us, it leads to dark thoughts, and this is where we're really at risk for saying harsh things or doing things we don't want to do—offending people, hurting our relationships, or getting silent and withdrawn at the exact wrong time. Or we may feel desperate and act out impulsively, or lash out. These symptoms might seem like just behavior issues, but you can see now how they begin with dysregulation.

After an outburst, a lot of us have a phase of *not* feeling or of not being able to show feelings. It's as if they've been partitioned off from our awareness, and in that state (dissociation), we sometimes behave coldly to the people we just offended.

My son's preschool teacher once got angry because, when she told me about some bad behavior of my son's that day, I had a blank expression on my face. It looked to her like indifference, and she accused me of not caring about my son, when really, it was entirely the opposite: I cared so deeply (I was mortified) that I dissociated and my face went blank.

These reactions don't necessarily happen because anyone is bad or selfish or weak, though we all have some weaknesses. These reactions happen in us—or they're made worse—because the brain is dysregulated. Nobody knew this before—not doctors, not therapists, not preschool teachers. Nobody knew why we reacted the way we did and why we were the way we were. And people judged us for it just as much as we judged ourselves.

But now we *know*. It's dysregulation.

CREATE A LOG OF YOUR EXPERIENCES OF DYSREGULATION AND RE-REGULATION

In your journal, begin to make notes that will help you notice and remember your own tendency to dysregulate—when it tends to happen, what it feels like, and what helps you re-regulate. As you continue noting these experiences each day, your pattern of dysregulation will become a little more visible to you. This is also a good tool to help you identify what your triggers are, which you'll be working on in Chapter 5.

Pay attention to moments when you become frustrated, overwhelmed, emotional, confused, forgetful, or checked out. If you can notice when these feelings occur, ask yourself if something may have triggered dysregulation. Make a note of it, and then later, when you're able to feel calmer, more centered, and re-regulated, make a note of that too.

Here's a format you can use: In your journal, go to a fresh page, draw a line down the center, and note the headings. One side is about what dysregulated you, and the other is what helped you re-regulate. Write as much as you like; brief notes over several days will help you see the pattern and may help you identify your dysregulation triggers.

WHEN DID I GET DYSREGULATED? WAS THERE A TRIGGER? WAS IT FROM SOMETHING EXTERNAL OR WAS IT A FEELING/MEMORY? WHAT DID IT FEEL LIKE?	AFTER THIS HAPPENED, WHEN DID I BECOME RE-REGULATED? WHAT HELPED? WHAT DID IT FEEL LIKE?
When I accidentally broke the coffee maker this morning, I got intensely angry and kicked the cupboard door. I felt frustrated, hurried. Also despair that everything we buy gets ruined.	I was flustered for about an hour. It stopped when I walked up to the mailbox; being outside made me forget that I was angry. The sun felt good.
I got to work late. So ashamed. Made everyone wait and had to rush right into meeting, then couldn't find the handouts. So flustered. Snapped at Lisa. More embarrassment.	Co-workers were supportive about my presentation. When they said that, I felt calmer. Took long brisk walk at lunch, shook it off. Wrote some fears and resentments till I could think again.
Sadie said I was being too intense and hung up on me. Felt both angry and desperate to get her to talk to me again (but didn't call, phew). Got really overwhelmed. Forgot to eat dinner. Cried.	Crying seemed to help! Felt sad but regulated.

WHY IT'S SO IMPORTANT TO LEARN TO RE-REGULATE

The goal of re-regulation is for you to feel good more of the time—to feel steady inside and mentally clear, attuned to what's going on around you. Being regulated helps your emotions to be an authentic response to people and experiences, not mere projections from the past. Being regulated helps your stress response to be "right-sized" so you can build healthy connections with people and not just attach instantly or push them away. Being regulated can help you detect red flags before you let destructive people into your life.

Some people say being regulated feels like all their brain cells have come back online, or like their senses have come back to life.

It feels *good* to be regulated. And here's a little secret: You already know how to do it! The next step is to get better at it. It takes practice, but you can start feeling the difference right away. You can go for what makes you happy and stop doing things that cause you problems. You can contribute to the world the way you were meant to contribute, without that extra layer of drama and confusion that has undermined your progress and keeps tearing you down.

You've probably, by instinct, craved calm and focus all your life. This capacity to regulate your nervous system and emotions has always been part of you. When you learn to access it, transformation of every part of your life becomes possible.

Learning to Re-Regulate Is Part of Life

Think of a newborn baby who is in distress. Their skin is red, their muscles are rigid, they arch their back, and they cry desperately. Newborns haven't yet learned to regulate, and this is what it looks like. When a parent holds and feeds them, they quickly calm themselves, shifting from desperate, dysregulated crying to a calm, comforted, alert state of re-regulation.

I remember witnessing the change in my own children when I nursed them as babies. I intuited that they were "disorganized" in their bodies when they were hungry or distressed, and that somehow the food, the touch, and the loving, face-to-face attention from me would re-organize their bodies. The word for this is *co-regulation*, and new research shows that all people—adults and children, and even animals—will often match others' level of regulation (or dysregulation).

This is why a lack of attentive care can harm normal development of the child's nervous system and self-regulation. It's also why parents who are themselves dysregulated may struggle to help a child to self-regulate. A vicious circle can happen: The child cries frantically, and the parent becomes more dysregulated, which further agitates the child, no matter how well the parent takes action to comfort them. Their nervous systems *feel* each other. People often ask me how they can help dysregulated children and family members, and my answer is, first, to master re-regulation yourself. I've also provided tips at the end of this chapter to help another person re-regulate.

Now that you're aware of the feeling and you've connected it to symptoms that result from dysregulation, you may be having an aha moment. Now things get exciting!

You may also have begun to notice dysregulation *everywhere*— in yourself; in friends, family, and co-workers; in strangers on the street and famous people; and even in fictional characters from literature. It's true! Something you thought was a personal failing can now be released as a normal symptom that's not your fault, knowing that healing is happening now.

Let's go over what we've already covered about dysregulation and what it is:

- Neurological dysregulation is a core symptom of early trauma that drives most other trauma symptoms. Its role in CPTSD has only recently been acknowledged.

- Though everyone gets dysregulated sometimes and eventually re-regulates, people with CPTSD get dysregulated more easily and stay dysregulated longer than the general population.

- Dysregulation is caused by a trigger—a stimulus from outside yourself (like a loud noise or a friend who keeps interrupting you, for example) or from inside yourself (a memory, a thought, or a feeling of physical pain, for example).

- When you're dysregulated, there are some signs you can feel—physically, mentally, and emotionally—and others you can't.

- Learning to notice dysregulation and to quickly re-regulate (and stay regulated) is the most powerful way you can advance your healing.

Re-Regulation Basics

Mastering re-regulation sounds difficult, but it's a skill you build, one positive step at a time. It's a set of actions and it's a life-style. You'll learn what helps you the most—and find the motivation to be persistent—by following the steps below.

1. Use your Daily Practice every day, twice a day.

2. Use your journal for the next few weeks to track when you get dysregulated and how you became re-regulated (see page 65 to review the instructions). When you discover new triggers or re-regulation strategies, be extra sure to write them down.

3. Exercise for at least 20 minutes each day, outdoors if possible. Run, walk, or do whatever you are able, briskly enough to elevate your heart rate and break a sweat.

4. Read and keep handy the Emergency Measures to Re-Regulate list below, and (if it's relevant to you) Tips for Helping Other People Re-Regulate.

EMERGENCY MEASURES TO RE-REGULATE

1. NOTICE WHEN YOU ARE DYSREGULATED! Are you flooding with emotion? Adrenaline? Panic? Say to yourself, "I'm having an emotional reaction." This is a good time to slow down and be gentle with yourself and others so you don't say or do something you'll regret later.

2. BE SAFE. This is not a good time to drive a car. Pull over and take your time. If what triggered you was an argument, use gentle words to stop the interaction for now, like "I want to continue this conversation, but I need to take a breather to calm down." Or, if you don't want to tell the other person that you're triggered, tell them you need a bathroom break, or if you're on the phone, say you have a call on the other line. Don't get into a discussion about it—just find a way to put the conversation on pause.

3. BUY SOME TIME. Separate from the other person if you can. Go to a room by yourself, even if it's the bathroom. No one has to know what you're doing. If it feels urgent, take even longer before you try to resolve anything.

4. STAMP YOUR FEET. You'd be amazed how helpful this is to bring yourself back into present time, in your body. As you stamp each foot, say quietly to yourself, "Right. Left. Right. Left." This helps your brain begin to re-regulate.

5. TAKE 10 DEEP BREATHS, focusing particularly on the out breath.

6. PRESS YOUR TONGUE TO THE BACK OF YOUR TEETH. This is a strategy to get back in your body.

7. SIT DOWN AND FEEL THE WEIGHT OF YOUR BUTT IN THE CHAIR. This is another strategy to get back inside your body.

8. EAT SOMETHING. When you're stressed, you'll probably crave carbs and sugar, but it's protein foods that will help you get grounded again.

9. WASH YOUR HANDS and feel the water and soap on your hands. Warm water is particularly calming.

10. **GET A GOOD, SQUEEZING HUG.** If no one is around, press your back into a corner and wrap your arms around yourself so you can feel pressure all around your torso. We're wired to calm down when we're hugged!

TIPS FOR HELPING OTHER PEOPLE RE-REGULATE

Getting dysregulated is like yawning. When one person does it, it's hard not to do it too, especially if the dysregulated people are those you live with. As a pair, family, or group, you become something like a neural ecosystem where one person gets set off and starts running around reacting to things, and soon everyone's getting set off.

It's not always easy to tell that someone is dysregulated. You may find yourself getting tense and dysregulated without even realizing why. This can be one strong sign that someone else has become dysregulated first. In people you know well, you probably have noticed some telltale signs. Here's what to do to help them (and what others can do to help you when you get dysregulated):

- Stay present. Pay attention to them and hold your focus calmly with them.

- Slow down. Don't use fast speech or sudden movements. Use a calm voice.

- If you want to open up communication, you can say things like "It seems like maybe you're getting dysregulated. Do you need us to make things calmer?"

- Don't talk a lot. It's good to pause and be quiet so they can talk, or recalibrate in silence if that's helpful.

- If you do need to talk, keep it simple. Don't introduce a lot of new information. No lectures.

- Don't keep asking if they're okay or asking what they want. Ask once, and then wait until they request attention or help from you.

- Don't "get in their head." Don't explain to them what you think their dysregulation is about or try to give them a science lesson. It's important that each person has room to figure things out for themselves.

- You can ask if they'd like a squeezing hug, but if they say no, let that be no big deal.

- Respect their physical space. Keep a little distance between you, and ask before you touch or get closer: "Do you want me to come sit with you?" Be willing to avoid touch if touch seems to trigger them.

- If things are tense or heated, you can suggest a five-minute break. Say it without anger or a threat. Suggest a plan for coming back together so you don't trigger abandonment buttons.

- Be patient. Don't take their actions personally.

- Focus on yourself while you wait for them to re-regulate. The best time to talk about dysregulation and what each person finds helpful is when everyone is regulated and calm.

In this chapter we covered many of the neurological aspects of dysregulation. In the next chapter, I'll teach you how to identify your triggers and begin working to calm them. And then in Chapter 6, we'll apply these lessons to emotional dysregulation and how to heal it.

CHAPTER 5

IDENTIFYING AND HEALING YOUR DYSREGULATION TRIGGERS

In our culture, the word *triggered* often means "upset" or "offended." But for our purposes here, a trigger is something that happens within you or outside of you (a stimulus) that causes you to become dysregulated.

Triggers are the connection between what happened to you in the past and the ways these wounds express themselves in your life today. Your past trauma generated the triggers, and your triggers set off dysregulation, which in turn sets off disconnection and self-defeating behaviors.

In this chapter I'll help you identify your dysregulation triggers and begin the work of calming them. When you are less triggered, you have more freedom to be yourself and do the things you enjoy.

A second option for you is to avoid your triggers, which is sometimes sensible but not always possible (for example, if your trigger is the sound of your baby crying), and it isn't always desirable (like if you are avoiding people altogether).

Triggers develop, almost as if they were installed, in response to trauma wounds: Something traumatic happened, and your nervous system remembers it and associates it with a person, a place, a feeling, or something as minor as a smell. When the trigger is activated, your nervous system responds as if that original trauma is happening again, prompting the release of stress hormones and then (because trauma has altered your stress response) neurological dysregulation.

Not all your trauma wounds installed triggers, and not all triggers can be clearly traced to a particular experience. It's not necessary to figure out the origins of all your triggers. What is important is that you learn to notice when you're triggered, so you can work on calming your response.

You won't always feel the trigger when it happens. Rather, you'll notice the feeling of dysregulation as it rolls through your nervous system. You might feel your heart begin to race or a rush of adrenaline—or you'll suddenly feel wooden and numb, unable to finish a sentence. You might feel a surge of anger so strong you want to scream—or you feel so panicked, you get the urge to quit your job, pick up a cigarette, or beg someone who has hurt you not to leave. Triggers can also make you freeze up . . . or feel nothing.

Most of what you feel when you're triggered is dysregulation, which temporarily has control of your nervous system: You don't have access to your full ability to reason, protect yourself from danger, or use caution in your words and actions. This is where you are prone to retraumatize yourself by pushing people away or avoiding them as a crude means to avoid getting triggered. Or you may lapse into other self-defeating behaviors that, very temporarily, help you calm mental and emotional chaos.

You can't undo what happened in the past. And you can't make other people, let alone the world, stop being so triggering (though, God knows, we've all tried!). But when you eliminate or reduce your reaction to triggers, very few of your trauma symptoms activate. Our focus in this chapter is to identify your triggers and begin work to calm them.

DO YOU HAVE THESE COMMON TRIGGERS?

Remember, in our context, a trigger is an event (within or outside yourself) that causes you to become dysregulated. The thing that triggers you could be something you hate (like getting yelled at), or it could be something you enjoy (like finding out you got a promotion). The problem is that it sets off dysregulation, which in turn sets off disconnection and self-defeating behaviors in you.

You may never have noticed the connection between a trigger and your response. For example, getting criticized may trigger you to become emotionally dysregulated and lash out at a loved one. Feeling hurried might trigger neurological dysregulation that makes you trip on the rug while getting ready for work. Several people talking at the same time might trigger a dysregulated panic response that makes your heart race. Feeling lonely might trigger you (in a dysregulated state) to eat a whole bag of chips.

IDENTIFY YOUR TRIGGERS

Below is a set of questions about common triggers. Take out your journal, and as you read, write whether you experience that trigger; what it feels like when it activates; and strategies you might use to calm that trigger. If you don't have a given trigger, it's fine to skip the question.

On page 79 there's a longer list of triggers; you'll have the opportunity there to rate your own triggers and identify those that affect you most.

People, Groups, and Isolation

- Which people (individuals or groups) trigger you? Why?
- What are some clues when you're in social situations (or alone) that you're triggered?
- What are some strategies to stay more neutral?

Abandonment

- Do you feel that you overreact (compared to a non-traumatized person) to the feeling of abandonment—for example, when you're rejected by someone, left out of a group, or waiting for someone who is late?
- What happens to your mood, physiology, and thinking?
- What people or situations set off your abandonment trigger?
- The next time you notice the abandonment trigger beginning, what can you do to keep it from becoming overwhelming?

Hurrying and Overwhelm

- In what situations do you find yourself hurrying?
- Does hurry trigger dysregulation? What is it like?
- What percentage of your time/activities is diminished by a feeling of hurry and overwhelm?
- What workarounds could you use to reduce the intensity of the dysregulation?
- What would help you get re-regulated faster in these situations?

Speaking Up or *Not* Speaking Up

I define speaking up for yourself as asking for what you want, or defending yourself when doing so requires courage on your part.

- Do you ever speak up for yourself when you are *fairly regulated*?
- What happens—do you dysregulate?

- Do you ever speak up for yourself when you are *already dysregulated*? What happens?
- Do you ever *not* speak up when you feel like you should? Why or why not? Does fear of dysregulation play a role in how you handle it?
- List some strategies you can use to speak up in a managed way, so you can do it without dysregulating.

Talking about Trauma

- What happens when you tell people about your traumatic experiences from the past? What does it feel like?
- Have you ever regretted sharing this information with anyone? Why?
- When you've kept your past trauma private, has it ever created problems?
- To help you be close to people and *also* stay regulated, what might be some good guidelines to give yourself around whom to tell, when to tell, and how much to tell?

Being Ignored

- In what situations have you been ignored or overlooked? Is it a trigger for you? How does it affect you?
- Have you ever overreacted to getting ignored? What happened?
- Do you have a pattern of putting yourself in situations where you get less than your share of listening and support?
- What strategies can you use to express yourself and ask for what you need in a way that's appropriate and calm enough that others give you an okay level of attention?

RATE YOUR TRIGGERS

Now that you've reflected on ways some of the most common triggers affect you, review this longer list of triggers and follow the directions for choosing your answer for each column.

Not all triggers are equal. Some are harmless, and some may severely impair your life—limiting your ability to work, connect with people, and feel joy. In this exercise, you'll have the opportunity to identify the triggers that *most need* some healing work and prioritize them accordingly.

In column A, on a scale of 0 to 3, note how much or how often you experience the trigger (0 = not at all, 3 = all the time).

In column B, on a scale of 0 to 3, note how negatively the trigger affects your life (0 = not at all, 3 = very negatively).

In column C, multiply the score you gave in column A with that in column B. Your total will be somewhere between 0 and 9.

COMMON TRIGGER	A: HOW OFTEN SCALE OF 0–3	B: HOW BAD SCALE OF 0–3	C: TOTAL SCORE MULTIPLY A&B
Isolation			
Abandonment			
Hurrying			
Overwhelm			
Feeling overlooked			
Feeling left out			
Feeling judged			
Feeling condescended to			
Feeling treated unfairly			
Talking about past trauma			
Speaking up			
Failing to speak up			
Others' dysregulation			
Large crowds			
Being in groups			
Getting stood up			
Feeling distrust			
Feeling lied to			
Being around drunk/ high people			
Making a mistake			
Asking for help			
Closeness with loved ones			
Showing emotions			
Lack of sleep			
Driving			
Public speaking			
Setting boundaries			

Saying no			
Embarrassment			
Sex			
Touch			
Violent/scary TV/films			
Being suddenly awakened			
Feeling jealous			
Not belonging			
Not understanding something (when others do)			
Feeling trapped			
Feeling unwelcome			
Feeling incompetent			
Feeling accused			
Defending yourself			
Physical pain			
Bad dreams			
Asking for what you want			
Not getting what you asked for			

Identify Your Priority Triggers

Now review your scores in column C and circle any values of 7, 8, or 9. These are your priority triggers.

TRIGGER ACTION PLAN

Once you've identified your priority triggers (they happen often, and/or they cause the most problems for you), write them in your journal, one at a time. You can think ahead and decide how to handle each of the triggers in the future by answering these two questions for each trigger you've identified:

- Can you avoid the trigger? If so, how?

- Can you calm your triggered response? If so, how?

Here is what your notes might look like:

PRIORITY TRIGGER	CAN YOU AVOID IT? HOW?	DO YOU NEED TO CALM IT? WITH WHAT STRATEGIES?
People drinking	No. I can't NOT go out with co-workers for client dinners, and I can't tell teammates they are not allowed to drink.	Need a way to feel less triggered at work dinners. Do Daily Practice before I go. Stop blaming co-workers for making me uncomfortable. They are doing nothing wrong. Check in with my friend who does the Daily Practice before and after.
Stop-and-go traffic	Yes. If I leave for work either earlier or later, I can avoid the stress of traffic.	If I do get stuck in traffic, I'll focus on taking deep breaths, and remind myself "This is only stress. It will pass."

You can't control all triggers or all of your reactions. But making a plan for how you will manage triggers has just restored your sovereignty over healing dysregulation!

YOUR MORNING ROUTINE

You've now learned about neurological dysregulation and the triggers that set it off. You're doing the Daily Practice, and you've started a journal. Your next step is to fold your practices together into a morning routine.

A morning routine has tremendous power to help you get regulated and stay more regulated throughout the day.

You've probably noticed already that your state of regulation goes up and down. Some days go well and you stay pretty regulated, and some days your mind is going all over the place—and not necessarily because anything triggering happened to you. Sometimes it just comes from within.

I need a morning routine both to lift my energy and focus, and to stave off the feeling of overwhelm that tends to visit me first thing in the morning when I'm vulnerable to dysregulation from within.

If I don't use my morning routine, the feeling that "it's all too much" can take over my nervous system. I can safely go get a cup of coffee, but then I need to write and meditate, stretch, and shower first thing. If I attempt to look at my phone or the news or all the little notifications waiting for me, it can completely capsize my day and make me foggy and distracted for hours.

I do the routine on bad days like a medicine, and I also do it on good days as prevention. Doing it regularly helps me to be habitual, automatically re-regulating when I touch pen to paper. This is how I set the tone of my day. If you like, you can create your own routine. Here's what mine looks like:

1. Wake up by 6 A.M., get up out of bed, and make the bed.

2. Feed the cat, make a pot of coffee (I like it, but I know not everyone does). Drink a glass of water and stretch for 5 to 10 minutes while I wait for the coffee to brew. On an ambitious day, I might I do a few squats and some easy push-ups on the counter, and on a

really big day, I'll do a sun salutation or two that I learned in yoga.

3. If the weather is decent, I go stand outside for a couple minutes—I'll stay on my porch if it's raining, but I just like to take a look at the trees and the sky and smell that good morning air.

4. Do my Daily Practice—writing fears and resentments while I sip my coffee, then meditating in a cozy chair with a blanket, giving my mind a rest and being open to inspiration.

5. Set my intentions for the day, noting things I want to get accomplished.

6. Open my laptop and take a look at my kanban board,˙ where I already planned the day last night. I revisit the tasks and the color-coding I use to indicate how long I think each task will take, and make any adjustments.

7. Take a shower, and finish with two minutes of cold water (a brisk reset for the nervous system!).

8. Get dressed, make breakfast, and sit down and eat while I read and respond to e-mails, review YouTube comments, and only *then* read the news. I have to set a timer, because I easily lose track of time when I'm on the Internet.

9. Wash my dishes and tidy the house (tidying is wonderfully re-regulating).

10. Walk briskly for 20 minutes outside and then sit down to work at 8 A.M.

˙ Kanban is a visual project-management system that a wide variety of productivity apps use. The one I use is called KanbanFlow. It's simple and inexpensive.

That's my morning routine. It takes about two hours between waking up and starting work at my desk (my commute is the 20-foot walk from the back door of the house to my studio and office). Occasionally I have to skip parts of my routine, because something on my schedule demands it.

I try really hard *not* to look at my phone or computer before I've done steps 1 through 7. It's tempting to see if any news or messages came in overnight, but this is something I learned from one of my mentors, Brendon Burchard: An e-mail inbox or list of texts is basically other people's agenda for me, and if I don't set my own agenda first, *their* agenda can take over my whole brain (or day) and put me right back into overwhelm.

I also learned from him to make my plan for the next day before I go to bed each night. That way I know when to be suited up and ready at my desk. This is a good habit, but it also makes it safe not to look at my phone or laptop first thing in the morning.

You may be worried that my routine sounds like too much for you—which it is for me too sometimes! I stick with it though, because it strengthens me against hard times and helps me to be happier and more myself.

You can create and customize *your* morning routine; it can be as simple or complex as you like, but it helps to keep it simple when you're first getting started. Be sure to incorporate your Daily Practice, morning and evening, and if you can, your dysregulation/re-regulation journal. The rest is up to you.

As you find your groove, you may also want to add things like praying, stretching, exercising, avoiding phone and computer until after your morning routine, having tea or coffee, reading inspiring literature, stepping outside, deep breathing, making a gratitude list, a cold end to your shower, a "calm" breakfast (low carb, with protein, sitting down).

FOR YOUR JOURNAL

• • • • • • • •

- Draft *your* morning routine. Try to keep it simple and doable.
- Which of the items in your morning routine are most important to do daily, and which are optional?

DAILY PRACTICE ASSIGNMENT

You have three choices about triggers: You can try to make people (or the world) stop triggering you; you can avoid triggers; or you can practice calming your triggers. The Daily Practice helps you to see your options more clearly and to sense which choices are right for each circumstance.

When you do your Daily Practice today, just keep naming the fears and resentments that are "up" for you. You don't have to make it all about triggers, but since you've been reading this chapter and noticing your triggers, it wouldn't be surprising if they made an appearance in your fears and resentments.

Just write it as it comes and be sure to sign off and meditate. Stick to doing this twice a day. You will very likely begin to notice moments of dysregulation and re-regulation in your day. This is preparing you for the next chapter, which is about one of the most important trauma symptoms to heal: emotional dysregulation.

CHAPTER 6

EMOTIONAL
DYSREGULATION

This is the trauma symptom that can damage your life more than any other—emotional dysregulation. *We* don't necessarily notice when it's happening, but other people sure do!

There's this idea out there that to heal the wounds of trauma, you have to "feel your feelings." We get told that we need to explore what we feel, trust what we feel, and feel *more* of what we feel—which may be true for some people. But for people with CPTSD, it may be the worst advice possible. Emotional dysregulation sometimes includes losing touch with our emotions, but more often it can drive us to feel them *way too much*. When this happens, the brain's emotional center (right front cortex) lights up, while the reasoning center grows dim. We can become *unreasonable*.

If you haven't yet learned to emotionally re-regulate, your life can be dominated by your emotions: Your relationships are dominated by your emotions. Even your career is dominated by your emotions. And being so emotional—having feelings that are inappropriately intense, or getting emotional at inappropriate times—can (and probably has) cost you the love and trust of more than a few people who were important to you. Simply "feeling your feelings" will not solve the problem. In this chapter, I'll teach you how to recognize when emotions are going off the rails and what to do to stop the damage and bring your brain and your emotions back into balance.

HOW TO TELL WHEN YOU'RE EMOTIONALLY DYSREGULATED

When you've lashed out or abandoned relationships because you were dysregulated, you may have felt as mystified as the people on the receiving end of these actions. Something happens . . . and it triggers dysregulation. You can almost feel the chemical change running through your blood, like a toxic drug.

Emotions come surging up, out of proportion to what's going on, or at an inappropriate time—like crying at work, or unleashing an angry outburst on your Internet provider when you call to find out why you have no connection. Your thoughts swing around like a wrecking ball: Where will they go? It barely matters to you when you're emotionally dysregulated, because (you believe) you've been *wronged*.

Sometimes when you're emotionally dysregulated, you'll have a big spike in feeling (in an argument with your partner, for example), and then after you've said hurtful things . . . you feel nothing; a numb state of dissociation can come over you. Both states—feeling too much or nothing at all—can lead you to say and do things you don't really mean: things that frighten and hurt the people on the receiving end. It can be hard to face, but this is how your trauma becomes other people's trauma. Until you learn to re-regulate, what unfolds from this dynamic destroys relationships and makes your trauma wounds worse. That's why healing emotional dysregulation is the most powerful thing you can do to stop the damage and allow trauma wounds to heal at last.

Here's an example. Let's say you have an argument with your partner because he forgot you had friends coming over to dinner, and you cooked, but your partner is late. Your friends have arrived and you've been trying to pretend everything was fine, calling and texting your partner three or four times—but he hasn't gotten back to you. Finally, an hour into dinner, your partner walks in. The moment he sees everyone there, he remembers the plan and feels flustered and embarrassed.

"Where *were* you?" you ask.

"I'm so sorry," he says and turns to the guests. "I knew you were coming, and I was really looking forward to seeing you. And then I got a phone call from this angry client at the end of the day, and I guess I just totally forgot we were meeting."

Your friends are happy to see him and reassure him it's fine, and they all start talking. But for *you*, it's too late. Old feelings (probably from being ignored and abandoned as a child) are welling up out of the past and filling your chest and your head. You briefly feel ashamed, because you've done this before and it's hard to make it stop, but then the anger is too big and it leaks out in little digs and weird vibes. You can't help it. And it *feels* like you're controlling your anger, but really, you're just delaying the horrible outburst that's about to start. People can *feel* your anger and dysregulation, and they will instinctively want to avoid you. So the guests say pleasant things and thank you for dinner and leave just as soon as they can. You turn to your partner, and all your anger comes rushing out: "You ruined the whole night!"

In the moment, it feels like these intense emotions are *the only rational feelings* a person could have, and your words turn vicious against him. But in reality, he merely made a mistake. It was rude, but a mistake nonetheless, and everyone else was okay with it and ready to enjoy the evening. It was your *reaction* to the situation that ruined the evening. Later, you will recognize this, but right now, the pain you experience *feels* like your partner is causing it, and it feels necessary to lash out at him.

It's moments like this when emotional dysregulation can drive you to say things you don't mean. The hurt and disappointment escalate into a toxic state of mind—almost as if you're in a trance, where no one cares about you and nothing is any good, and you genuinely believe you've been a fool not to see it sooner: The relationship must end!

So you say it's over, or you make the threat, and even if your partner is used to this and sticks around, this kind of behavior gradually drains away the love that brought you together, cutting off the depth and sweetness that would otherwise be growing over time.

This is what I mean when I give the side-eye to the idea that all we really need is to "feel our feelings," or "grieve," or get in touch with our anger, or whatever nontraumatized people do when their emotional lives are hard. That's not always what's needed. For some people with CPTSD, *what's needed is to self-regulate*, using work-arounds to protect our relationships from these outbursts while we do the healing work that changes our lives for the better.

You'll find that if you can control the emotions before they get intense (and you may have a very short opportunity to do that), you can avoid a lot of the problems that come from over-reactions and overwhelm, and it's easier to get back to a calm and regulated state.

I have a friend who visualizes emotional dysregulation as an airplane taking off, and regulating this is what she calls "keeping the airplane on the ground." I love that.

WHAT TO DO TO RE-REGULATE YOUR EMOTIONS

Here are some steps you can take to calm your emotions and keep *your* airplane on the ground. You *can* stay regulated, even when you're upset, if you understand what's happening and you practice, practice, practice.

- When you go into a strong emotional reaction, notice it's happening. Are you feeling scared, angry, overwhelmed? Is adrenaline quickening your heartbeat? Are you starting to cry? Say to yourself, "I'm having an emotional reaction."

- Slow the interaction *down*. If it's a conversation with someone that is triggering you, pause, think, prepare to see things in a new way. Sometimes, simply slowing things down can reduce the overwhelm, and less overwhelm means you can recover your perspective on the situation and experience a little calming effect inside.

- If you're about to cry and you don't want to because, for example, you're at work, you're giving a speech, or you don't want to be vulnerable in a particular situation, here's a trick I use. Imagine a knob on your belly, sort of like the gas knob on a stove, and it goes from 1 to 10. Think of the knob as a valve on your emotions, where you accidentally left the knob at eight, and so you dial it down to just two. Your emotions are still there, but they're at two.

- If anger is what's overwhelming you, you can use what used to be called "restraint of pen and tongue." That means don't say anything or call or e-mail or send a text *while* you're angry. If you already know you are prone to emotional dysregulation, then what feels like a little venting for you might cause you to say and do things you don't really mean and that you'll later regret. Instead (because it's important to express yourself) promise yourself you'll express yourself later, when you're calm. If the other person knows you're angry, your workaround is to find a gentle, polite way to postpone any more conversation.

- If your need to express yourself feels urgent (but there's no true emergency), it's probably best you take extra time before saying anything. You can do this even if the conversation has already started. If you feel yourself dysregulating, your workaround is to say kindly, "I'm getting a little worked up, and I don't want to make this into a big, horrible thing. I do want to talk, though; can we come back to this in thirty minutes (or tomorrow)?" Very few conversations are so important that they can't wait a little while.

  Before you have that conversation, take out your paper and pen and get some fears and resentments on paper, and ask for them to be removed. Remember, you are not stuffing these feelings down; you're just naming and releasing them so that whatever might be "extra" can go, leaving you with the ability to say what's fair and true. This way you're more likely to be heard and understood and to get the kind response you'd like. The great thing is, you can write your fears and resentments just about anywhere—in the bathroom, in the dark of a movie theater, in the car, in bed in the middle of the night, or even at a desk while you pretend to be working. I've done this, and I know it's not ideal to fake-work on the job (and in some kinds of work it's impossible), but sometimes a little writing and releasing is the best way to get focused, calm, and productive again. It's definitely better than having an emotional meltdown!

- Use the Emergency Measures to Re-Regulate from Chapter 4. In particular, get some hard exercise (you can run up and down a flight of stairs, or at least walk around the block). Quick steps that help are to take 10 deep breaths, or drink a glass of water. Wash your hands or take a shower—a cold shower if necessary, or hot, then cold. Do whatever it takes to give a little jolt to your system and break the trance, as if you're saying to yourself, "Come on, let's get you out of this dysregulated state!"

- If you like, you can talk with a person who is not, in that moment, in a conflict with you. This should be someone you trust to help you get some perspective. I don't recommend trying to tell a long story—not when you're already upset—because talking about it can trigger dysregulation even more. Pay attention to what happens when you talk about what's upsetting you. Are you getting more emotional, or talking faster and faster or louder and louder, or trying to *convince* the person of your position, rather than just saying what it is? This is not only a sign you're further dysregulating, but you now may be triggering dysregulation in the person listening to you as well! Our nervous systems talk to each other like that. It's better to talk less, listen more, and pay attention to your friend's state of regulation, which can help you find your state of regulation.

- Remember, everything that needs to be said can and should be said, but not necessarily in that moment. If you possibly can, wait until you're regulated again, feeling calmer and more lucid and able to feel the range of feelings you have about someone (and not just rage). If you feel frantic to be understood, it's another clue to pause and postpone communication until you are calm and more likely to be understood.

- When you're feeling regulated but the intense thoughts start fluttering in, just keep reminding yourself to hold the thought and instead focus on next steps—positive actions, positive words. This isn't positive thinking or "toxic positivity." This is redirecting your thoughts to clear a mental space—something with less emotional charge where you can anchor yourself. You're not suppressing your feelings, just postponing expressing them until you're a little more regulated.

- Contrary to popular belief, you don't *have* to talk things out to *get* regulated. Talking about your feelings is important, but there's a time and place, and sometimes that best time and place is *later*—when it will be helpful and constructive, and when it will help you have and keep the relationships with loved ones that you treasure, even though it doesn't feel like that when you're emotionally dysregulated.

- When in doubt, go back to the first tip: reminding yourself, "I'm having an emotional reaction." Then use your tools so you can refrain from venting or lashing out. Your feelings will be there waiting for you when you're calmer and no longer dysregulated. Then when you express yourself, you can do it elegantly, with fairness and love. It'll feel great to keep your relationships gentler like this, to get past the shame of overreactions and to enjoy the way your connections with other people—rather than getting ruined—begin to deepen and get better over time.

FOR YOUR JOURNAL
• • • • • • • •

- What signs tell you you're becoming emotionally dysregulated?

- What have you done in the past to become more regulated? Has it worked?

- If you've ever become emotionally dysregulated, has it harmed your relationships? Your career? Your health? What happened?

- Which of the tips in the list above would you like to try? Give them a page in your journal that you can easily find the next time you need to re-regulate your emotions.

HOW TO ACHIEVE "EMOTIONAL SOBRIETY"

Emotional sobriety is a term they use in 12-Step recovery, and I remember the first time I heard it, it scared me, because it sounded like something I would never be able to *do*. Yet I knew in my bones it was something I needed and even craved.

My problem wasn't ever substance abuse, though; it was Child-hood PTSD. And though I didn't have a name for it when I first started healing, I knew that whatever was wrong with me was very much like being an alcoholic or drug addict. I was exhausted all the time. I was late to things, I got angry easily, I was sad a lot. I thought it was just me, and I felt ashamed because I really had no idea how to change. So the feeling I got from the words *emotional sobriety* was both intimidating and hopeful. Whatever it was, I wanted it.

In substance recovery, *sobriety* means more than just "not drunk" or "not high." In recovery, *sober* means living in a frame of mind and an emotional state that is even-keeled and nondramatic, which helps prevent relapses. This is because an emotional upset or even an intense positive emotion can be the very thing that triggers a relapse.

If you've ever had any kind of addiction, you know that it's the continued abstinence that can be the hardest. So staying sober can really depend on guarding against experiences that are going to be emotionally upsetting or intense—at least during early sobriety. And that probably means avoiding the slippery behaviors that can open the door to intense emotional experiences—things like getting into a fight, or having a one-night stand, or letting yourself get too lonely, or getting into sneaky activities of some kind that make you feel ashamed (stealing or lying, for example). Addicts are encouraged to keep life gentle and not too crazy, since intense emotions could drive them to take a drink or pick up a drug.

But what about for people with Childhood PTSD, who are prone to emotional dysregulation? It's not an addiction, but it does have something like relapses, where our emotions go from grounded and right-sized to dramatic and oversized. With drugs and alco-hol, either you consumed it or you didn't. Our relapses may be harder to define.

In my opinion, an emotional relapse can be defined as when you override considerations of safety, consideration for others' well-being, or your own best interests. Whether it's an avalanche of negative emotions; a discombobulated, spaced-out feeling; or a state of hyperexcitement about money or romance—if it causes us to stop taking care of ourselves, we can call it a relapse.

Now, dysregulation obviously is not the same thing as intoxication, but it can mimic that lack of clear judgment, that volatility, or the complete lack of boundaries that you'd see in someone who's drunk or high. And trauma and addiction are definitely related, in that a history of trauma seems to have a high correlation with subsequent addiction. One distinction between addiction and trauma is that with addiction, the substances themselves are the active agent. You consume them. You get drunk or high.

With trauma, there's nothing quite parallel to that. The active agent is seldom something you consume. It's an experience or behavior that functions as a trigger. It could be an emotional flashback that appears as soon as you wake up, or it could be a stranger who yells at you. The trigger sets off a physiological reaction that you can't directly control or avoid. So without any conscious behavior from you, you can slide into a dysregulation "relapse."

As people with Childhood PTSD, is there anything we can do to *prevent* episodes of emotional dysregulation and instead cultivate emotional sobriety?

The first thing is to be guarded around negative thinking and emotions that could be a slippery slope into oversized negative feelings. It's possible to notice you're feeling sad or angry without getting stuck in those feelings. Most of us were conditioned to explore negative feelings when they arise, but as I explained earlier in this chapter, some of us need to hold those feelings lightly, perhaps writing about them but not talking about them too much—or least not until we're regulated again.

When it comes to healing painful memories, there is such a thing as healthy compartmentalization. Small upsets might be safe to feel, but we might need to hold big upsets at a bit of a distance sometimes. It's possible to look at a tough situation and not open your heart to it 100 percent.

Of course, it's not healthy to *always* shut down around painful feelings: That's denial. But having a little bit of control over when to embrace the feelings and when to be more circumspect is a good thing. That's part of emotional sobriety.

To some degree, you can avoid triggers. When you're working hard on healing from trauma, it may not be the time to start a new relationship or run for political office! It's a good time to engage with activities that are calming for you: exercise; being outside in nature; avoiding high-conflict, high-drama people; and avoiding the news are all strategies you can use.

When you're triggered, an ordinary feeling like anger can froth up into rage. Now you're on thin ice emotionally. With CPTSD, rage can easily burst out into saying something that you'll regret, followed by three days of intense dysregulation. Or, on the other end of the emotional spectrum, the trigger could be a positive emotion like elation or giddiness—triggered by something that feels thrilling or exciting, like when the person you weren't sure likes you finally texts you, or you get a surprise check in the mail.

With emotional dysregulation, elation can be strong enough that it causes you to relapse just as hard as if you had a rage attack. It starts as good news, but the resulting dysregulation can throw you into depression, anxiety, brain fog, or romantic obsession. So emotional sobriety means being mindful about things that are emotionally intense for you, good and bad.

You can (for a time) avoid experiences likely to trigger you, while you simultaneously learn to calm your reaction to triggers. As you're healing, you will sometimes have a strong emotional reaction, then a period of neurological dysregulation followed by a period of getting back on your feet again. When it happens, you can use the experience as practice. Sometimes the victory is that you got out of your slip and you didn't let it slide into an avalanche of dysregulation.

Falling down and getting back up is practice, and it's how you'll learn to use your tools to handle stress in a better way.

It's impossible to *completely* avoid triggers. Life is full of them. You can't just stop going outside, stop working, or stop waking up! But you can focus on noticing and arresting the reactions that are likely to snowball as a result of your trigger emotions. And here is where you can reference your worksheet on triggers from the last chapter. For you, the trigger emotions might be fear, abandonment, anger, a feeling of injustice, or a feeling of being excluded, for example.

Shame is a big trigger for emotional dysregulation. It starts with "Oh, I think I may have said something I shouldn't have said," which can escalate very quickly to "I'm a worthless idiot, and I'll be alone forever!" This kind of self-attack can then lead to hurtful behavior toward others, which can lead to more self-attack (or retaliation from them). Dysregulation makes the feelings go out of control, growing larger and spreading all over until they don't even make sense in the context of what happened.

So, emotional sobriety is the state where you've become skilled—not at denying your emotions but at halting the *progression* of emotions from an ordinary, right-sized level to a full, Incredible-Hulk-ripped-T-shirt reaction. Having some control over this takes time and practice. It involves talking to people who are on the path of healing or ahead of you, learning from them, and learning to tolerate the times when you fail. Part of this healing cycle is getting back up on your feet and trying again.

It may bother you sometimes that while *you* are exercising emotional restraint, other people are allowing themselves to go emotionally crazy. They can yell, they can rush into a relationship, they can stay home and eat ice cream in bed all day, and nothing bad seems to happen. Don't let this fool you into throwing away your emotional sobriety. Even people without CPTSD do better when they pause and temper those impulses.

For *you,* pausing is everything. It takes self-discipline to avert the intense reaction, but the more days you live through where you haven't freaked out on someone or made an impulsive decision, the more you have an inner equilibrium that makes it easier to pause between trigger and reaction.

How to Stay Emotionally Sober

Just like with alcohol or drugs, it's easy to get cocky and think, *I haven't jumped into an instant and ill-advised relationship in two years. I think I can handle jumping into this relationship that's right in front of me today!*

We all know what happens then. The same, old thing—only sometimes even worse than before. In AA they say that alcoholism is progressive and fatal. A person might not drink for many years, but if they relapse and drink one time, they often find that the drinking has progressed, i.e., it's worse than ever before.

It's my experience that emotional sobriety is vulnerable in the same way. You haven't raged at another driver in a long time, but then your defenses get weak one day and you end up pursuing someone down the road, leaning on your horn.

The old shame and dysregulation may come back, but when you're healing, pain can tell you what you still need to heal.

When you notice you're in the danger zone with the "gateway emotions," you can take immediate steps to back out of it. Don't make big decisions or pronouncements until you've had a chance to run them by a trusted friend. Use your Daily Practice twice a day, without fail. Use your emergency measures to re-regulate—exercise, take a shower, suck a lemon wedge—anything that helps you give a little nudge to your nervous system with a sensation, a movement, a reminder that you're working to heal these old reactions.

Other people might tell you you're doing it wrong or insist you need to feel your anger, grieve, or go deeper into your emotions. Ask yourself: Does the person suggesting this have Childhood PTSD or know about the role of dysregulation in driving trauma symptoms? Because as much as they're trying to be helpful, they may only know what works for them. You're learning what works for *you*.

The triggers in life never stop, but as you heal, you'll meet them with grace and strength.

FOR YOUR JOURNAL
•••••••••

- Do you relate to the idea of emotional sobriety? What does sobriety feel like for you?

- If you could stay emotionally sober more of the time, would it change your life? How?

- What does it feel like when you lose your sobriety? What actions or experiences triggered this?

- What actions have you taken in the past to stay "sober" emotionally? Did they work?

- Identify tips from the list above that you'd like to try next time. Devote a full page (or more) in your journal to list those tips, and make them easy to find when you need them.

DAILY PRACTICE ASSIGNMENT

In your next Daily Practice, notice the emotions that appear in your fears and resentments, and allow them to be removed (or released) along with your thoughts. Keep using your Daily Practice, as it will help you clear emotional "buildup" each day.

Beginning to heal all the ways you become dysregulated is the most powerful preparation you can do for the next step in the book—healing the feeling of disconnection.

CHAPTER 7

DISCONNECTION

Childhood PTSD is, in essence, an injury to the ability to *feel connected*. What's simple for most people—being in a group, having a friend, feeling a sense of belonging, or recovering from a conflict with a co-worker—can be fraught for us. The sense that we are somehow separate from everyone—even when we're at a party, even in a marriage—is an almost universal feature of life for people who grew up with neglect and abuse. Sadly, *feeling* disconnected often results in *being* disconnected, and it can generate its own set of problems that make connecting with people even harder.

This is the most tragic part of unhealed Childhood PTSD—to be capable of love but to be unable to sustain normal connections. It is a devastating price to pay for what happened to you as a child.

If you're like most people with CPTSD, social interactions are loaded with dysregulation triggers. Unconsciously, you may have been managing those triggers by avoiding people. Now that you are learning to re-regulate, you're already beginning to calm the triggers and heal the connection wounds that once made "peopling" something you had to limit. And more healing is possible if you are intentional about it.

This is a vulnerable phase of your healing work. There are bound to be painful memories and a temptation to rationalize your difficulties, deny your power to change, shut down emotionally, and flee from social situations.

And yet full healing *now* requires you to learn to connect with people anyway. It is through practicing *within* relationships (of all kinds) that you can build your capacity to connect, listen to, and love others, and to finally develop a sense of belonging. It gets easier when you recognize that many of your connection challenges are related to past trauma and can be healed.

With the mastery of re-regulation and a stronger and more consistent ability to connect with others, you'll slip less often into old, self-defeating behaviors that sabotage relationships (those behaviors will be covered extensively in the next chapter).

In this chapter, I'll teach you the signs that trauma has affected your ability to connect. I'll describe the feeling of trauma-driven disconnection and separateness—what causes it and how it can make you resist people and groups, even when you long to be included in them. And finally, I'll give you tips to overcome ruptures in connection so you can sustain happy relationships even when you feel triggered, and even when there is conflict.

SIGNS THAT TRAUMA HAS AFFECTED YOUR ABILITY TO CONNECT

While these symptoms are not exclusively related to trauma, they are common for those of us who grew up with abuse and neglect. There are no right or wrong answers, and there's no score, but your *yes* answers suggest areas where past trauma has affected you.

- When you participate in a group—where some of the other people are friends and feel connected to one another—do you struggle to feel that *you* are a part of that group?

- Do you feel sad or bitter that people don't give you the help, recognition, or appreciation that you deserve?

- Do you sometimes feel like other people got an instruction manual for how to live life, but you've had to figure things out for yourself?

- Do you find yourself avoiding social engagements simply because it's triggering to be around other people?

- Do you consider yourself socially awkward?

- Is it a pattern for you to say hurtful things to people that damage your relationship with them and then regret it later?

- Have people said you talk too much or are a poor listener?

- Do you work hard to listen to others and to support and encourage them, only to find that most people in your life never reciprocate?

- Are your relationships more superficial or shorter-lived than you'd like?

- When you express your opinions or feelings, do you often fear you said too much or offended people?

- When you sense that people have pulled away from you, are you often unsure why?

- Do you feel as if you get treated differently than most people, with less love and less inclusion than you deserve?

- Do you hold friends and neighbors at arm's length, fearing if you let them in, it will hurt or overwhelm you?

- Do you find yourself mostly in unequal friendships, where one person has more power or influence than the other?

- When you make a new friend, do you live in fear or "wait for the other shoe to drop," expecting the friend to eventually abandon you?

- Are you haunted by a fear that you will end up alone in the world?

FOR YOUR JOURNAL

●●●●●●●●

- Which of the signs listed above have you experienced?
- How severe is the impact of these symptoms on your life today?
- Are there any signs you used to suffer with but have healed from?
- If you felt 50 percent more at ease with people, would that change your life?

HEALING IS POSSIBLE

Some feelings of disconnection stem from a temporary state of dysregulation, which can resolve as you learn to master re-regulation. Some may be from developmental wounds, where neglect prevented the full development of your natural capacity to connect, and these can take longer to heal.

We know that abuse and neglect early in life can literally change the brain and restrict the normal cognitive processes that enable us to (a) seek out and connect with good, appropriate people, (b) know how to interact with them successfully, and (c) detect red flags so we can avoid people who should *not* be let into our lives.

Many people with Childhood PTSD have spent their lives suppressing a sense of dread that they'll always be alone and they'll never be truly loved. It's okay to grieve that you were robbed of your birthright to be well-enough loved and properly guided into the web of human connection that's all around you. Your fear of letting people be closer to you can be so strong that you may be tempted to isolate yourself as a way to stay "safe."

Safety is necessary sometimes. But you need more than that to heal the isolation and loneliness that is such a big part of trauma's legacy. Whether you long for connection but can't seem to keep good people in your life, or you have avoidant tendencies and go to great lengths to keep people away, it's highly probable that early trauma is part of the reason.

In a way, this is good news, because the healing work you're doing right now is helping to drain past trauma of its power over you. You are well on your way to forming happier, closer connections with the people you want in your life.

ARE WE DISCONNECTED BECAUSE WE'RE DIFFERENT?

No matter what happened to you or what your symptoms are, you are not defined by Childhood PTSD. You are a whole and precious human being with the same needs, feelings, and dreams as anyone else.

But many of us have trouble shaking the sense that we're somehow *different*. It can seem like everyone else knows how to act—what to say and how to be connected—but *we* never got the instruction manual. It has made many of us feel alienated and hopeless, as if nothing we could ever do would make us belong.

First of all, you do belong. You belong here on earth, whether you feel it or not. This is your world just as much as anyone's.

Second, those of us who had trauma as kids *love* the feeling of belonging that we find with each other. There are things about our experience that only other people with Childhood PTSD understand, and those who use the method of healing that you are now using have especially good insight about the path you are walking. They are walking it too.

We are more alike than you know, and if you'll have us, we hope you'll consider yourself part of the tribe!

And yes, we've all wondered too: *Are* traumatized people actually different? The answer is yes, in some ways.

You may have grown up feeling different because you were *in fact* different from most of the other kids you knew. Maybe your family came from another country, or you knew you were gay, or your family was poor compared to others you knew, or your parents were unusually strict. These are real differences. When other kids were getting pep talks from their parents about the nuances of interacting with people—what to do and not do—your parents may have left you to figure it out for yourself. Or they may have suffered with disconnection themselves and couldn't model for you how to make and nurture friendships.

If there was trauma happening at home, that's a big difference too. Maybe you didn't feel like you could bring friends to your house because it was dirty or run down, or you never knew what kind of drama might be going on when you walked in the door. That'll make you feel different—and it's one reason why so many of us always gravitated to other kids (and later, adults) who were also traumatized.

What we've lived through has changed us. If you've ever felt that nontraumatized people are on some "group wavelength" that *you* can't seem to access, as if you have the wrong password to the Wi-Fi, there might be some truth in it. Attunement to nonverbal communication can be damaged by trauma too. This is part of why we often feel a bit clueless in social situations.

You may have felt different for as long as you remember, or you may not have noticed it until your teens or early adulthood. Sometimes we only notice that we're different after we've completely exhausted other theories about why connecting was hard for us. We thought it was all about a particular school or a particularly mean kid, for example. Those of us who had a social difference from other kids (like having strongly religious parents or being a different race) may have believed that *that* explained the deep feeling of difference.

But after enough time, we noticed that it couldn't be *just* that, because there was a pattern; we felt separate almost everywhere, even with people just like ourselves. No matter how nice we were, or how eagerly we tried to fit in and make friends, we still had trouble connecting—or forming deep and lasting connections, anyway.

DISCONNECTION IS A SYMPTOM, NOT A CHARACTER FLAW

You may have blamed yourself for the ways that connection is hard for you. It's not your fault you were traumatized as a child and it's not your fault that this impaired your ability to have close friendships or a loving partnership.

Our ability to connect was first injured when we were exposed to extreme stress or deprived of the one-on-one closeness and interaction that is so important for children's learning and emotional development. There's nothing any of us could have done to prevent what happened.

Dysregulation, too, can cause the disconnected feeling, and it can drive you to lash out, cling desperately, or otherwise strain your connections with people close to you. It can also propel you to break off relationships simply because your dysregulation has been triggered (and we'll talk about this later in the chapter). Sadly, for people with unhealed Childhood PTSD, behaviors that hurt your relationships just seem to "slip out" and feeling that you can't control this may discourage you from trying again.

This sense of disconnection is like other aspects of Childhood PTSD, where even professionals have misunderstood why we acted the way we did. Some thought we were bullies, or rude, or avoiding connection on purpose (and eventually, many of us do become avoidant). But in the beginning, we were just innocent kids who needed love, who wanted to hang out with other kids, like all kids do. And for reasons we couldn't figure out, we seemed to be screwing everything up. In the eyes of people who didn't know about childhood trauma, I can see how our disconnection seemed like a choice.

You may have been labeled defiant or promiscuous or antisocial, or called even worse names by your peers. And yes, we each have some negative personality traits, and it's possible they have played a role.

But what if the problem was just brain changes from past neglect? Wouldn't that be enough to explain why it was hard to grasp social rules, read people's intentions, and understand nonverbal communication? Wouldn't that, all by itself, be enough to make connection feel hard?

Like other aspects of CPTSD, disconnection is something we can heal with practice. We work on calming triggers, healing the nervous system, and mastering social skills we didn't learn at home. You might always be a little sensitive, a little quick to withdraw, a little overreactive, and that's okay. You don't have to fit in with *everybody*, and you don't have to connect with people just because you think that's what you're supposed to do.

A good goal is to connect enough to have a few good friends, a loving partner if that's your heart's desire, and if you have children, enough attunement to be a good parent. You are a one-of-a-kind person, and part of your healing includes accepting who you are.

FOR YOUR JOURNAL
· · · · · · · ·

- Are there ways you feel different from other people, or disconnected from them?

- Have you discovered any connection wounds that you once thought were character flaws? How does it feel to learn these symptoms are normal?

- Imagine what it would be like if you had enough healing that you could form (or heal) relationships of all kinds with ease. What would change about your life?

THE STRUGGLE TO BELONG

Like everyone, most of us with CPTSD want to be included in groups, but in many cases, we find it hard to *feel* like we're part of them.

You might join with enthusiasm, then get uncomfortable (or resentful) and pull away. Maybe you think that the problem in each case is that *other* people exclude you, and sometimes that could be true.

But the telltale sign that semi-participation is your choice (even when it doesn't feel like it) is that you almost always situate yourself at about the same distance from the center of the group— meaning the group's most involved and influential members. They are the inner circle, and all around them are people with a little less involvement and influence, and around *them* are people who are on the periphery; they want to keep a connection to the group but have one foot out the door and may leave if things feel uncomfortable.

That was me. I used to always like to settle about 80 percent out from the center—invited to the party, but not responsible for making the party happen. A lot of times, I'd start out motivated and thinking, *This group is great! I've finally found my people! I want to be involved with this!* And then I'd move toward the center of the group, take on a more active role or maybe even a (gasp) leadership role! And then sooner or later (usually sooner), I would find some reason to pull back. I might go to about 40 percent out of the circle first, but eventually, I'd bounce out of the group altogether. Being part of something was—and in some areas of my life still is— uncomfortable for me. So, why is that?

I used to think my trouble with groups was just one episode of bad luck after another—the wrong co-workers, the wrong mom's group, the wrong 12-Step friends. I'd think, *These people don't get me, so I must not belong here.* And I never saw that it was a consistent pattern until I had some healing from dysregulation and started to have some clarity.

Can we just admit it? People are triggering! And a group of people (for us) is a whole *bunch* of triggering people. It is understandable that groups are hard for us, because when you have the sensitivities of Childhood PTSD, groups can feel like an assault on your senses. They can activate deep and painful memories about not belonging and not fitting in. It feels personal and permanent, like a high school experience that never ends.

The need to be included in groups is not a weakness. It's primal. We are born into community, and as much as we want to escape it sometimes and be independent, we never can, not really. Evolutionary biologists will tell you it's a survival strategy so that you have warmth and food and protection from predators and so on.

But it's not just biological. Inclusion is important for the growth and development of your being, your intellect, and your spirit. Without inclusion in human relationships, the process of becoming *you*—the blossoming of your real self—is arrested. It can't fully happen in isolation, and fulfillment never arrives.

Participating in groups is how you become *included*. It takes tremendous courage for some of us. People will trigger and offend you sometimes, and you'll get dysregulated, and it may be tempting to flee. But I encourage you to push at least a little on the edges of your comfort zone so you can grow a support system of people who care about you and who can come to your aid if you're broke or lonely, or feeling like your life is falling apart. Though you've probably had to do it before, you're not meant to go through all that alone.

You can agree to bring something to a potluck dinner, join a choir or take a quilting class, or invite friends out for a hike. When you show up for people in your life, you grow less fragile and more flexible, more connected, and more included.

DON'T WAIT UNTIL YOU FEEL "HEALED" TO BEGIN CONNECTING

When you're feeling bruised and ostracized from a lifetime of disconnection, you may find it hard to admit openheartedly that you *need* people and that you want to belong. You may rationalize your avoidance by saying that staying isolated is just for now, until you heal.

And sure, some healing may need to happen before you can fully enjoy connected social relationships, but right now, you need people in your life so that you *can* heal. Connection is medicine. Your personal growth needs some friction, some contact with people to show you where growth is necessary, and to give meaning to your life. Everyone needs this.

If you allow isolation to take root long term, it will take over, and your very worst traits will have a huge, fertile space to grow. People in isolation grow crabbier, less empathic, more bitter, and more paranoid. And then it gets harder to turn the ship back toward connection again, because you've gotten too eccentric, too awkward. Have you ever felt this beginning to happen to you? Have you seen it in other people? I really noticed it in myself when lockdown was ending and I began to spend more time with people again. I was rough on the edges—a little angry, a little edgy.

Confining yourself to the periphery of life may feel like good boundaries helping you keep from getting hurt or dysregulated. And for some badly traumatized people, complete isolation is their self-preservation, at least for now. Yet not sharing yourself with other people is an emergency-protection measure, not a way to live your whole life.

It's risky to connect with people, but the reward is that you get to be included. And included is secretly where we all want to be.

PRACTICE CONNECTION A LITTLE EACH DAY

Even if you're a long way from healing broken connections with the people in your life, you can make small acts of connection as you go through the day. You can try this with people you already know, as well as acquaintances or even strangers. The goal is to make connection a ready habit and to start with little steps that are easy.

I invite you to choose a small act of connection and do it! Here are some examples.

- Stand outside your house and give an easy hello to the next person who passes by.

- Get on social media (if you use it) and "like" 10 friends' posts, just to help them feel someone cares.

- If you see it's a friend's birthday, write them a note.

- When you pass someone on the sidewalk or in a public place, give them a warm smile.

- If a friend tells you about something they're excited about or struggling with (for example, a new pet or a dreaded doctor visit), take an interest. Listen and ask questions. By paying attention, you show you care.

- With that same friend, follow up with a text or a call the next day: "Just wondering how it went at the doctor," or "I was thinking of you and your puppy and hoping his first night went well!"

- Express gratitude to the people who are working to help you, such as grocery checkers, receptionists, teachers, and food servers. Let them know you appreciate their kindness and help.

- Be extra patient on the phone with customer service workers. If there's a mistake or misunderstanding, instead of showing frustration, reassure them that it's okay and work with them to solve the problem.

FOR YOUR JOURNAL
• • • • • • • •

- Which of the tips above would be good next steps for you to try?

- Which ones feel like too much, at least for now?

- When you do try to connect with people (for example, taking actions like those listed above), does it trigger dysregulation?

> - When social interactions dysregulate you, what does that cost you? For example, do you end up isolating? Does it hinder your productivity? Has it caused you to avoid social invitations and opportunities?

BUILD YOUR CAPACITY FOR CLOSE AND TRUSTING RELATIONSHIPS

Connection wounds don't just keep us from forming relationships. They can make us feel disconnected in relationships we *do* manage to form, romantic and otherwise, and activate self-defeating behaviors that drive us right back into disconnection. In the next chapter, we'll take a deeper look at those behaviors, but in this section, I'll walk you through some immediate strategies to rescue or repair relationships that you may not have learned in your family of origin.

You can take these measures when things are tense, or when you fear you've blown it already by pulling away, lashing out, or cutting off people you actually want in your life.

The first step is to get honest with yourself about your current circumstances and what is likely to happen if you don't learn to connect with people better. In your mind it will seem like there's an external reason for why you *must* pull away or argue or isolate yourself again. You'll find yourself making excuses not to show up on time, or convincing yourself that people are all terrible. But really, you're just trying to manage your tendency to get dysregulated, and now you have better ways to accomplish that.

Dysregulation is neurological; it's happening in your brain and body, and it can distort your perception of how difficult or easy it would be to talk through the stressful moments with a friend. You may be rusty at it, but it gets easier with practice. You can go slowly, creating boundaries that help you, learning to prevent conflict before it starts and to heal conflict when it's already happening. It's okay to be imperfect at this; even tiny efforts can help you move in a positive direction.

Here are some tips:

LEARN TO NOTICE WHEN YOU'RE DYSREGULATED AND BUY SOME TIME. Your mind will tell you that you *must* fix things, change the relationship, or make some kind of decision. But this is a terrible time for that. You may need some time alone to get re-regulated, so promise yourself you won't say or do things *in the heat of the moment* that will cause hurt. Remind yourself that anything important can be decided tomorrow.

WRITE YOUR FEARS AND RESENTMENTS THE *minute* YOU ARE ABLE. You don't have to wait until it's "time" to sit down and write. Write as soon as you feel trouble kicking up within. The shift produced by the Daily Practice is sometimes dramatic and sometimes subtle, but either way it can bring tremendous emotional relief.

Sometimes writing will bring tears or a big feeling of release, as if the problem has evaporated. Sometimes it doesn't feel like anything big. All these responses are normal. Just let the Daily Practice do its work to relieve your stress so that your choices are visible to you again and things feel easier.

With practice, you'll create a little distance between a strong emotion and what you do about it. Pausing in that moment to re-regulate and think clearly can save relationships and change your life.

WHILE YOU'RE HEALING, "TITRATE" YOUR SOCIAL INTERACTIONS. *Titration* is a word borrowed from the field of medicine that describes the administration of tiny amounts of a drug, then pausing to check the response. If there is a negative reaction, you wait. If it goes well, you administer a little more of the drug. After testing these small amounts, one after another, you find the right dose. This is a good analogy for your efforts to connect with others—in small steps with pauses afterward to check how it's going, how you feel, and whether the interaction triggered some dysregulation.

For example, if you've been isolated but you reach out to an old friend, plan to meet only for coffee the first time. Afterward, you can use your Daily Practice to process how that went, and then re-regulate. If it went well, consider having lunch the next time, and see how that goes. You don't have to rush in and plan a big day together. Taking small steps first gives you a chance to "check the temperature," avoiding the feeling of overwhelm or getting triggered into old behaviors.

SET BOUNDARIES THAT HELP YOU STAY REGULATED. You may think of boundaries as a set of rules for other people to follow so that they don't upset or trigger *you*. But if your "boundary" is an attempt to make a fellow adult behave a certain way so that you feel okay, it's a *preference*, not a boundary. You can ask for what you want, but if the other person is not in agreement, or can't (or won't) comply, you get to decide what you'll do—step back, end the relationship, accept the person as they are, or pepper spray them in the face if necessary! Your boundaries are the things you're willing to do to protect your safety, your time, your sanity, your personal space, and your body from what you won't accept.

Some ordinary examples of boundaries might include not drinking alcohol, not working on weekends, or dating only people who are interested in marriage. At times when you are working hard on your trauma healing, you may want some additional, temporary boundaries, such as getting to sleep before 11 P.M., avoiding long visits with family members with whom you've had painful conflicts, or not talking about traumatic experiences with people other than a therapist or close friend.

When we're unclear about our boundaries, any kind of connection can feel threatening, giving rise to the urge to either control people or avoid them. It can also serve as a de facto invitation for people to walk all over us, leading to resentment and the urge to pull away. This ruptures connection, and if it isn't healed, it can grow into a lifetime of avoidance. That's how we run the risk of actualizing our greatest fear: that we will live our entire lives alone.

When you know your boundaries and can trust yourself to honor them, you don't have to fear getting stuck in social situations. You can get to know people, detect red flags, and gradually take steps to be closer, because you know that if things get weird, you'll step back out.

Creating boundaries and sticking to them is how you give yourself the freedom to keep yourself safe *and* connect with people you want to get to know.

TAKE RESPONSIBILITY FOR YOUR FEARFUL REACTIONS. All your life, you may have been managing dysregulation by avoiding social situations that triggered you. With healing, you now have another option: You can work on your reactions, let other people be themselves, and stay to enjoy the interaction with people who would be good and safe to have in your life.

An epiphany comes when you accept that your triggers are generated not by the people around you, but from *within yourself.* Even if you could make other people change (which is unlikely), your fears and resentments would still pop up, and you'd be triggered. Your task now is to calm your triggers and to develop the discernment and confidence to gradually expand your circle of connection.

When you're bothered by someone, you can release the urge to *tell* them (in the moment, at least) how they bother you. Fear distorts your thinking, and it's easy to be unreasonable while triggered.

Instead of jumping in to blame others for how you're feeling, it can help to notice the triggered reactions you feel arising in you that in the past have pushed you into dysregulation. In these moments, you can work to get re-regulated (as always, your handy pen and paper will help you, wherever you happen to be). Whatever you say in a more regulated state is going to be very different from what you'd say if you spoke up *while* all the fear was upon you.

Your fears and resentments are the natural "residue" of living your life and all you've been through. They are normal. They're a form of stress release. With practice, you'll find it's easier to release them than you think. In a calm and lucid state, you can choose to get closer or to let go. You can express yourself or keep quiet. You can set a boundary or open your heart. But you never again have to blow up the situation just because your feelings had no outlet and you got overwhelmed.

If you do get into a conflict with someone, you can now handle it in a new way, so that honest communication and repair of the relationship remain possible.

LEARN TO PAUSE A CONVERSATION THAT'S GETTING HEATED. When anger boils over and a conflict threatens to escalate, there are ways to get through it without using abandonment, the silent treatment, or rage. Here's what to do:

1. Acknowledge to yourself that you can feel yourself getting more and more emotional or dysregulated.

2. Ask for a short break (5 to 15 minutes). If you and the other person are close and they know you get dysregulated, you can explain frankly that you can feel you're getting dysregulated, and you'd like to pause the conversation so that you don't say things you don't mean or hurt them unnecessarily.

3. If it's a less intimate relationship, you can give another reason for the break (e.g., you need to make a phone call or check your e-mail).

4. Tell the other person when you will return to finish the conversation (e.g., "15 minutes from now") and then do actually return.

5. Avoid criticizing the other person or blaming them for your dysregulation, even if you feel that they caused it. Blaming them will only escalate the argument, and the goal right now is to de-escalate it.

6. Focus on keeping communication open and caring and avoiding the need to leave or go silent.

7. If you do take a break, use your tools to re-regulate (e.g., the Daily Practice or Emergency Measures to Re-Regulate on page 69).

WHEN YOU'VE HURT SOMEONE, APOLOGIZE. A full and heartfelt apology has the power not only to mend the relationship, but to make your life full, happy, and purposeful and help to heal shame and low self-esteem. Here are the steps to give a "clean" apology:

1. TAKE TIME TO PREPARE YOUR APOLOGY. In-the-moment apologies are good too, but if you have time, get clear first about what you did that you feel needs an apology. Run it by a trusted friend if you can, to make sure you're taking the right amount of responsibility (not too much, not too little).

2. WRITE YOUR FEARS AND RESENTMENTS ABOUT THE SITUATION. With less fear and resentment, you have more capacity to see what's going on and what needs to be done about it (if anything), and you'll probably find you have more empathy for the other person and for yourself.

3. TAKE NOTES TO REVIEW THE DETAILS OF WHAT YOU DID, and write how you would feel if you were in your friend's shoes. (Hurt? Embarrassed? Betrayed?)

4. PLAN HOW YOU INTEND TO DO THINGS DIFFERENTLY FROM NOW ON. Be honest with yourself about this. Don't be unrealistic or just say what you think you should say.

5. MAKE YOUR APOLOGY. Contact the person involved and let them know you'd like to apologize about something. This helps them psychologically prepare and decide if they're willing to see you. Meet face-to-face if you can, or by phone or video meeting. Use text or e-mail only if that's the only way.

6. MENTION ONLY YOUR OWN ROLE IN THE PROBLEM AND LEAVE THEIR ROLE TO THEM. Don't say anything about their role. If they want to talk about it, they will (but prepare for the probability that they won't use the opportunity to admit what they did that hurt you). Maybe you're not ready to be close to the person if they don't apologize, and that's up to you. But you can at least clear up your role in the problem and stop feeling guilty.

Here's a formula for what to say:

1. SAY, "I'D LIKE TO APOLOGIZE TO YOU FOR (name what you did)."

2. BE AS HONEST AND ACCURATE AS POSSIBLE. They're more likely to hear you if you show you understand why it was hurtful.

3. DON'T MAKE EXCUSES like "I was under a lot of stress," "I was tired," or "You did it first!"

4. TELL THEM HOW YOU WOULD FEEL IF THAT WERE DONE TO YOU. You might say, "I know I would feel angry and betrayed if that happened to me. I'd feel worried about what everybody thinks."

5. DEMONSTRATE THAT YOU GET IT. Don't minimize. Don't grovel either. Your empathy here is the one thing that can really help the other person relax their hardened heart, listen to you, and open up to the possibility of healing.

FOR YOUR JOURNAL
• • • • • • • •

- Have you ever erupted in a dysregulated response and later regretted it? What happened?

- How do you feel about the idea that your triggered response comes from you and not other people?

- Do others violate your boundaries? How?

- Do you know what your boundaries are? Are you able to express them and honor them?

- Have you lost relationships you valued because of conflict in the past? Could that have been prevented? Is repair possible?

DAILY PRACTICE ASSIGNMENT

Facing your connection wounds can open old hurts and make you question your role in relationships that have been difficult or lost. Be sure to give yourself plenty of time to write all the fears and resentments that have surfaced, and then rest your mind in meditation.

Your Daily Practice will help you process old hurts, doubts, and annoyances that will naturally arise as you gradually connect with more people in a deeper way. Regular writing and meditation can help you build your confidence that no matter what happens when you connect with people, you'll be able to deal with it.

Healing your ability to connect is a day-by-day process that takes courage and persistence, but it brings rewards quickly, and it strengthens you for all the good healing work you're doing. You will discover a greater power within yourself than you ever thought possible—with a newfound resistance to the dysregulated, self-defeating behaviors that once blocked you from thriving.

In the past, it might have been impossible to reach this phase of healing. But now you have the Daily Practice and the certain knowledge that your newfound ability to re-regulate and connect will support you as you take the *next* step in healing that we'll cover in the next chapter—facing and naming the self-defeating behaviors that have held you back.

CHAPTER 8

"INSIDE" TRAUMAS AND SELF-DEFEATING BEHAVIORS

Like all CPTSD symptoms, self-defeating behaviors are activated by triggers, then exacerbated by dysregulation and disconnection. So all your work so far in this book has prepared you for this challenging but powerful step in your healing: when you face the things you *do* that keep retraumatizing you.

Few people talk about this part of our trauma; most therapy and literature focuses entirely on the things done *to* us—let's call them "outside" traumas—such as abuse and neglect by your parents, growing up poor, or being bullied by schoolmates, for example. The more outside traumas you endured then, the more likely it is that you developed "inside" traumas—things you believe and do in your present-day life that *worsen* the effect of the original traumas.

Inside traumas start as an innocent flight away from pain, but if they persist, they create more trauma and more life problems. They include things like repeatedly choosing bad relationships, undermining your career with dysregulated behavior, or smoking two packs of cigarettes a day (just to name a few self-defeating behaviors I know all too well). Inside trauma can be as harmful as, or worse than, what happened to us in the past, so it's important to face and heal this part of our trauma too.

Focusing on the way we retraumatize ourselves sounds to some people like victim-blaming. And you most definitely were a victim. But you are the one who can change your life today, and if you avoid this fact, you risk staying trapped in victimhood.

The trauma in your childhood is *not* your fault. It's also not your fault that it affected you all these years or that you've found it hard to change. Now, facing and healing your inside trauma is how you rise up and access your inner power so you can create the fruitful and happy life you deserve.

In this chapter, I'll show you common self-defeating behaviors so you can identify the ones that are active in your life and choose which ones are your top priorities to heal. And (this is one of my favorite parts of this book) I'll share a description of what it's like when your self-defeating behaviors are healing.

A BRAVE AND POWERFUL STEP

It can be hard to admit that we are the ones who sometimes make our problems worse. You've probably noticed this when you've tried to help someone who is defensive and stubborn about a mistake they've made.

You may have been criticized and invalidated so heavily in the past that it feels as if this admission could break your spirit. That's why I've reserved this chapter for this stage of your healing work in this book—because now you have knowledge and tools, and your spirit is strengthened and ready.

Everyone has self-defeating behaviors, but traumatized people tend to have *more* of them. Along with dysregulation and disconnection, these destructive behaviors are part of the "three-legged stool" I defined earlier in the book, the three areas where Childhood PTSD manifests in our lives and where we need to focus our healing.

When we take time to focus on the harm we've caused ourselves, we're not denying the harm that was done to us by others. If the people who hurt you were never held accountable, they should be. And I hope they apologize to you someday if they're still living.

But even if those people take full responsibility and apologize for what they did and make restitution, the trauma wound already happened, and the damage is done. You can examine the past, take legal action, write a book, confront your family, or even forgive them if you like. *But the only person who can heal your trauma wounds now is you.*

This is a turning point in your healing process: to grieve what was lost and what you deserved but never had, and then to step up to take ownership of your healing from now on. This is your time for *sovereignty.* You are in charge, and you decide what comes next in your life, including the level of commitment you will give to your healing from day to day and the methods you decide to try. You may consult experts like therapists and doctors and groups and books (including this book), but *you* will be the one to decide which behaviors and symptoms are priorities for you to heal and which ones you feel (for now at least) are healed enough.

PREPARATION TO LIST YOUR SELF-DEFEATING BEHAVIORS

On the next page, you'll find a list of inside traumas—common behaviors and attitudes that likely started because of outside traumas; they can become habits that hurt you, and sometimes other people too.

Some of these behaviors are serious and some are minor; it's usually a matter of degrees, and it's for you to decide if something is a problem that needs your attention. Some things on the list may seem much worse than any problems you have, but they can happen to anyone if conditions get rough enough. None of us is above the problems of life.

Some self-defeating behaviors harm only you; others harm other people. Most of them increase the odds you'll slip into other self-defeating behaviors, which tends to keep your life in a state of crisis, pain, and being stuck.

Whatever your behaviors are, the minute you acknowledge them, healing begins and choices appear. Where there is a choice, there is hope! It takes determination and it takes time, but no matter what happened in the past, you can stop repeating old patterns. You are born to heal.

Your self-defeating behaviors may be a little different from the ones shown on the list, but seeing them written down will help you name them, starting with obvious problems that you know are limiting you. As your healing progresses, you'll be aware of some of the more subtle ways you lose your bearings or thwart your own progress.

You may be tempted to make huge to-do lists or beat yourself up. There's no need to do either! All you have to do is read about self-defeating behaviors and acknowledge any that you feel are active in your life. You can make notes as you go in your journal.

I strongly recommend you use the Daily Practice after you read this chapter (or even while you're reading it) to help you easily face memories and process feelings that may surface as you think about your role in the problems you have today.

Common Self-Defeating Behaviors

- NEGLECT OF YOUR BODY. This includes wearing inappropriate, dirty, or shabby clothes; having poor hygiene; having an unsanitary, severely run-down, or cluttered living space. It includes the avoidance of necessary medical and dental care, neglecting to eat healthy portions of nutritious food, and avoiding physical exercise that your body needs.

- BLAME. This manifests as a difficulty seeing your own role in your problems or as slandering people to enlist others to think poorly of them. You may believe that you "attract" problem people, as if you have no role in choosing or attaching to them. Blame also includes victim thinking, bitterness, and the belief that all your problems are the result of a country, a race, racism itself, sexism, foreigners, a political party, religion, lack of religion, certain foods, your parents, etc. It also includes "beating yourself up" and blaming yourself excessively (or for things you didn't do).

- "CRAPFIT." This is my word for the trauma-driven tendency to fit yourself to unacceptable people and situations. It is a survival strategy learned in childhood, when you had no choice but to tolerate dangerous or negligent parenting. When this maladaptation is carried into adulthood, it can lead you to attach to bad partners, miserable jobs, and intolerable living situations. It often goes hand in hand with a paralyzing fear of abandonment.

- BLACK-AND-WHITE THINKING. Traumatized people are especially drawn to extreme views, groups, authority figures, or belief systems. You may find yourself frequently outraged at the news and even thriving on outrage to lift yourself out of depression. This may have cost you the freedom to peacefully disagree with others or to step away from conflict when it's in your best interest. You may find that you dominate others or are often connected to others who dominate, and this may have resulted in a loss of contact with family, friends, co-workers, or neighbors.

- NUMBING WITH SUBSTANCES. This refers to the use of drugs and alcohol in quantities, with a frequency or in a manner that damages your parenting, relationships, physical and mental health, career and finances, and the safety, dignity, and emotional well-being of you and everyone whose lives you touch. There are certainly people who can use drugs and alcohol with no ill effects. It is worth questioning, though, whether light use helps or hinders your trauma-healing work, especially given that intoxicants lower inhibitions and increase the likelihood that you'll act out on other self-defeating behaviors.

- ADDICTIVE USE OF MEDIA AND ENTERTAINMENT. This refers to the excessive use of TV and streaming media, Internet sites, games, and social media to the extent that it interferes with sleep, meals, daily routines, family responsibilities, work, school, and finances. It includes the time you spend looking at your phone, especially if you do this when others are present and expecting to interact with you (like at the dinner table) or if the time you spend robs others of time, attention, and support that they may rightly expect (as with a partner and children).

- DISHONESTY. This includes lying, stealing, infidelity, evasion of taxes and debts, and other ways of breaking the law. While there are exceptions to every rule, the test of dishonesty is whether you are trying to deceive someone (or a group or organization) who has placed their trust and good faith in you. It can also mean exaggerating, talking behind others' backs, saying nothing when someone has accidentally overpaid you, or hiding important facts about yourself (lying by omission) from people who deserve to know, such as not telling a partner or someone you're dating whether you're open (or not) to marriage or children, or if you're already married.

- WORK PROBLEMS. These may include chronically adversarial relationships with employers and co-workers, a pattern of staying stuck in unfulfilling work, and/or earning less than you need or than is fair. It may also include avoiding the education and skill development that your career demands for you to stay current or advance. For some, the problem is chronic unemployment or a pattern of getting fired, suing their employer, or getting sued.

- IRRITABILITY. This includes having frequent arguments and fallings-out with friends, neighbors, partners, and family. It includes ranting, road rage, hanging up on people, or blocking them at the first sign of conflict; mistreating others; and violence.

- EXCESSIVE FOCUS ON OTHERS. This can take the form of codependency, where you neglect your own needs and personal growth and instead pressure someone else to improve their life, believing that only this can make you happy. Other-focus can also take the form of people-pleasing, where you abandon yourself and try to make others like or approve of you (or stop abusing you).

- AN ATTRACTION TO TROUBLED PARTNERS OR FRIENDS. This is one of the most damaging self-defeating behaviors. You may find yourself repeating a pattern of relationships with partners who are emotionally unavailable (or literally unavailable, because they are married and must hide their relationship with you from others). It includes a pattern of relationships with alcoholics or addicts, or people who are abusive, controlling, or damaging to your other relationships or to your family and finances. This behavior often goes hand in hand with complaining (often on social media) that a loved one is abusive, narcissistic, or otherwise a terrible person, but staying in the relationship and rationalizing why staying is necessary.

- UNFULFILLING ROMANTIC LIFE. This includes wanting a relationship but never asking for or accepting a date; staying in bad relationships, or behaving destructively in your relationship (cheating on, withholding love or sex from, or denigrating your partner) but not leaving.

- **ABUSE OF SEXUALITY.** This self-defeating behavior includes compulsive behavior around sex; promiscuity; or presenting with an overly sexualized appearance and conduct in a way that hurts others and compromises your sense of dignity, emotional security, and ability to be honest and "real" around sex and relationship dynamics. It includes coercing others to do things they don't want to do, or tolerating coercion from others. A pattern of unintended pregnancies sometimes points to either coercion or dissociation around sex.

- **ROMANTIC OR FINANCIAL FANTASY.** These tendencies become self-defeating when they become a flight from reality—not being really "here" when things are tough, and consequently, a failure to take reasonable actions in the face of problems. Harmful romantic fantasy can include obsession or infatuation with someone who can't or won't be with you, to a degree that harms your happiness and your relationships and obligations personally and professionally. Fantasy can trigger the development of huge, unrealistic expectations that lead to making unfulfillable promises. You may inflate the importance of relationships, events, personal attributes, or career prospects.

- **AVOIDANCE OF PEOPLE, RESPONSIBILITY, AND PARTICIPATION.** In a crisis, withdrawing into social isolation can provide much-needed respite for an exhausted nervous system and frayed emotions. But as a long-term coping mechanism, avoidance will halt your personal growth and allow the worst in your personality to grow. Avoidance can take the form of procrastination or a refusal to commit to long-term relationships and fleeing when people grow close to you (or need your help). Avoidance can be covert, where you have people in your life but you're never quite present for them, or you hold people at arm's length. Avoidance can be subtle, too, like bringing nothing to a potluck or not returning calls.

- DEBTING. You may be living beyond your means to pay for a home, car, or therapy, believing that "somehow the money will arrive" but with only a vague sense of the path to solvency. This self-defeating behavior also manifests as foreclosure, gambling, bankruptcy, and even homelessness.

- REPEATING TRAUMATIC PATTERNS. Most people with Childhood PTSD have trouble in their lives that is similar to the original trauma. Those who grew up with violence in the home will often end up in abusive relationships. Those who were neglected will keep finding themselves with unavailable partners, unable to detect trouble or step back when trouble appears. When faced with problems similar to those you suffered as a child, you may find yourself going into freeze mode; relapsing into dysregulation; and feeling deep rage, anxiety, and reversion to old behaviors.

FOR YOUR JOURNAL
• • • • • • • •

- List a few self-defeating behaviors that most affect your life (they may or may not be listed above). Then, next to each one, assign a rating on a scale of 1 to 5, with 1 being "not very harmful" and 5 being "ruins my life."

- Is there one high-scoring behavior (harmful) that you are ready to change?

- What steps could you take in the next seven days to get started? Is there one step you can take today?

IDENTIFY THE BEHAVIORS YOU WANT TO CHANGE

On the next few pages, I'll guide you through an exercise to identify the behaviors that may be retraumatizing you. As you complete this exercise, you may be tempted to go to extremes—to attack yourself for being terrible in a thousand ways—or to deny there is any problem at all! Most of us do a little of both. Honesty means we admit a fault, but we try to keep it in perspective. None of us *asked* to have Childhood PTSD. Our behaviors are a normal response to terrible things that once helped to keep our minds and bodies safe. Now, if we're ready, we can start to change all this, get on track, and be free!

It can be scary to look at ways we may have let people down or limited ourselves, so go forward GENTLY at this step. Gentleness means we try to look honestly, but with compassion, hope, and even humor. With healing and some courageous effort, we trust that our faults will be fewer and our strengths will blossom.

SELF-EVALUATION: WHAT ARE YOUR SELF-DEFEATING BEHAVIORS?

Here are some self-defeating behaviors that are common in people who grew up with trauma. See the questions and instructions in "For Your Journal" on the next page.

- Neglect of body

- Blame

- "Crapfit"

- Black-and-white thinking

- Numbing with substances

- Addictive use of food

- Addictive use of media/entertainment

- Dishonesty

- Work problems

- Irritability

- Excessive focus on others

- Attraction to troubled partners/friends

- Unfulfilling romantic life

- Abuse of sexuality

- Fantasy

- Avoidance of people, responsibility, participation

- Debting

FOR YOUR JOURNAL
• • • • • • • •

FOR EACH OF THE BEHAVIORS LISTED ON THE PREVIOUS PAGE, ANSWER THE FOLLOWING QUESTIONS. REFER TO THE FULL DESCRIPTIONS ON PAGES 124–129 IF NEEDED.

- How often do you engage in this behavior?
- How harmful is this behavior to you or others?
- Does dysregulation play a role when you slip into this behavior?
- Does feeling disconnected or lonely play a role when you slip into this behavior?
- If this changed, how much would it improve your life?

NOW CHOOSE YOUR PRIORITIES FOR CHANGE.

- Of all the behaviors you've just considered, which one would you like to prioritize for change? Write it in your journal.
- If you want, you can choose more than one, but don't take on more than three to change at once. You can work on more behaviors later. If you're in doubt about which behaviors to prioritize, write your fears and resentments and see what happens.

DAILY PRACTICE ASSIGNMENT

When you face hard things, it's crucial that you use your Daily Practice to process the fearful and resentful thoughts that are inevitably tangled in painful memories. Make extra time today to write a little more than usual, and be sure to devote a full 20 minutes to restful meditation.

SIGNS YOUR SELF-DEFEATING BEHAVIORS ARE HEALING

Congratulations on the hard work you did in this chapter to face and prioritize behaviors you'd like to change. Before we move on to the next chapter, I want to leave you with a list of signs that your healing is in progress. Bookmark this page and check it periodically to see how many have come true for you.

WHEN YOUR TRAUMA IS HEALING, YOU NO LONGER TEND TO SEE THINGS— PEOPLE, YOURSELF, AND SITUATIONS—IN BLACK-AND-WHITE TERMS. You no longer hold them up as all good or put them down as all bad. You come to appreciate the complexity of things, the way people can have faults but be decent anyway. You have less outrage and more curiosity, less impatience and more persistence. You lose the attraction to extreme views or authority figures and gain the ability to interact with a variety of people. Relationships where one person dominates become either more equal or fade away entirely. It is less necessary to cut people out of your life. Think of all the struggle you've had in the past around this problem and how good it feels to be free.

YOU HAVE A NATURAL DESIRE TO CARE FOR YOUR BODY. Part of it is because you have less drama and more energy to do things like take a walk, floss your teeth, or shop for clothes that look good on you. You feel a little better, and so now, when you feel too schlumpy to leave the house or you're tired from watching TV until 1 A.M., it doesn't feel worth it anymore. It's possible to face your addictions and take action to overcome them. One little step after the other leads to more clarity and more enthusiasm for life, and you want to do even more good things for yourself.

YOU CRAVE HEALTHY FOOD INSTEAD OF JUNK. The effect of past trauma can lead to everything from obesity and eating disorders to a tendency to deal with stress by binging on carbs and sugar. These foods can be calming at first but dysregulating in the long run. And as you heal, you no longer want that feeling.

YOU'VE LOST THE DESIRE TO BINGE ON MEDIA, INCLUDING TV, VIDEO GAMES, AND LOOKING AT YOUR PHONE ALL THE TIME. These addictions once seemed more important than sleep, meals, doing your job well, or being present in your life. Now your devices are just tools, and you've been released from the compulsive need to use them.

YOU ARE NO LONGER TEMPTED TO FUDGE THE TRUTH. You no longer engage in behaviors such as exaggerating, hiding important information about yourself, or lying. There's nothing you need to hide or feel ashamed about! You don't have so many problems, so you're comfortable being more honest about what's going on in your life. Being yourself just feels better. You now experience real discomfort when you're *not* being real. You now *want* the truth to filter through your life, and if there's anyone still in your life who can't handle who you are and how you really feel, you can safely assume they're not meant to be there. When they're gone, even though saying good-bye was sad, there's now a big, nice space where someone who loves and accepts you can be.

YOUR WORK LIFE GOES BETTER. You no longer stay stuck in unfulfilling work. You've either changed your relationship to that job or gotten a new one. If lack of work used to be a problem, all the good changes happening make it easier to get work and earn money that supports you and the people who count on you. You know how to steer clear of exploitative or abusive employers. You've lost your appetite for conflicts on the job, and you've gained the ability to show up, do good work, be an encourager of your co-workers, and (when needed) be an advocate for yourself and your ideas.

YOU'RE NO LONGER INTERESTED IN ASSIGNING BLAME TO YOURSELF OR OTHER PEOPLE FOR PROBLEMS; YOU FOCUS INSTEAD ON FINDING GOOD SOLUTIONS. You feel less angry, less irritable. When something is your fault, it's easier to just own it and apologize. And when someone else owes you an apology, if they don't give it to you, you don't dwell on it. You no longer feel the need to make other people into your "projects" for improvement and instead find joy in your own healing and in changing your life. Blame-filled news and social media posts no longer appeal to you. People in your life may not know why, but they feel better about themselves when they're around you.

YOU'VE LOST THE ATTRACTION TO UNAVAILABLE PARTNERS AND TROUBLED FRIENDS. Connecting and bonding with (and *staying* with) people who brought trouble into your life once caused so much damage, but now there's no attraction. Instead, you are drawn to people who are stable and happy to be with you, and who make it easy to talk honestly and resolve conflicts. The spell of trauma is broken, and you are able to step away from people and situations that are unacceptable to you, rather than trying to control them. When you decide to get close to people, you can go slowly, share yourself openly, and feel okay, even when it's new and uncertain. You take pleasure in allowing others to be themselves; you no longer compare them to an "improved" version of them you hold in your mind. There is peace when you are single, and harmony in partnership. No matter how your relationship status changes, you feel loved.

YOU PREFER REALITY TO FANTASY. The tendency to check out by spending too much time in a fantasy romance or fantastical business success is common with people in the middle of trauma, but in the end, it's just another way to avoid real problems and needed actions. When you're healing, it feels less necessary, and when you catch yourself daydreaming, you come back easily to where you can actually connect with people and put your goals into action—which is here and now. You have time in your life for joy and friendship, strengthening you for a connected life.

YOU ARE COMFORTABLE IN GROUPS AND ONE-ON-ONE WITH OTHERS. Because you have boundaries and you know how to use them, you are free to accept invitations from others and to invite them to spend time with you too. You are willing to step away from people and situations that are not a fit for you. You become genuinely interested in others' experiences, finding pleasure in both listening to them and sharing your own story. You are close to people you respect and trust, and they respect and trust you. You find meaning and fun in your life through participating in groups; you are flexible to assume leadership roles at times, as well as to support others who lead.

YOUR MATERIAL WELL-BEING COMES TOGETHER IN A POSITIVE WAY. Most people in the world—including most happy people—live good lives without being rich and famous, and some live on very little money at all. Financial hardship can fall on anyone. But when you're free of trauma, it's more possible to earn a steady income, let go of get-rich-quick schemes, live within your means, and release the fear of the past (when maybe you were a few hundred dollars away from homelessness too many days out of the year!). At last, you have what you need.

It all gets better at the same time—a little here, a little there—when you have good tools to heal your CPTSD symptoms. You can sleep at night. You can handle hard days. You can hold your head up even though you make mistakes, because you're not sabotaging yourself in ways that make you ashamed. This is what healing feels like when you're not retraumatized all the time.

Even when progress is hard and slow, you are the sovereign healer of your own trauma wounds. You may decide to enlist support from a trusted friend, a support group, a 12-Step fellowship, or a therapist. It's good to seek out people who understand trauma healing and who walk the path of healing themselves. The best things we give each other are validation and encouragement, and then even when things feel heavy or like they are too much, we find a way to keep going on the path.

The path, we have found, is a long and ultimately happy one. In the next chapter, you will complete this cycle of healing (there will be many cycles, as long as you live). You've worked hard to face and heal your dysregulation, connection wounds, and self-defeating behaviors. Now it's time to discover and celebrate parts of yourself that have been stuck under trauma symptoms all this time.

CHAPTER 9

BECOMING YOUR
FULL AND REAL SELF

Here you are, having done the hard work in Chapters 1 through 8, and you've arrived at the happiest part of healing.

Millions of people around the world are still struggling with Childhood PTSD symptoms. For too long, the path to healing has remained out of reach for us—it was too expensive, too hard to find, and often didn't help.

This is tragic for each person, because it keeps them from becoming who they are *meant to be*—fulfilled, authentic, and able to build a loving and fruitful life. They live trapped by their own trauma symptoms as we all once were, heavy with sadness, suppressed by exhaustion, and dulled with brain fog. Like all people everywhere, we long to develop our unique gifts and share them with the world, but until there is healing, it's next to impossible. This is the trauma-shaped hole in our world.

The goal of healing isn't just to feel better—although you *do* need to feel better, and you can. And it isn't just to find love (though you probably will), or to get ahead in work (though that's very likely too).

The reason you need healing is to become the full, glorious, and real self you are meant to be, and to bring the gifts that *only you* can into the world. We need you, desperately.

CLEARING THE WAY FOR A BREAKTHROUGH

When my healing from trauma first began on that long-ago night, all I really hoped for was not to feel so sad, and this happened for me very quickly. What I didn't know at the time is that real healing and real happiness truly begin when we find the thing we're meant to be doing with our lives.

In the first decade of my healing, things changed quickly. I earned a master's degree, started a consulting practice, had two wonderful children and a very brief marriage with their dad, and a divorce. What took a long time was learning to connect with people and to take part in groups, and changing my self-defeating behaviors, especially around romantic relationships.

It was a long road, and 12 years after first learning the Daily Practice, I became embittered. My life as a newly divorced mother was harder and lonelier than I'd have liked, and it seemed to prove to me that the Daily Practice didn't work. So I quit using it.

Over the course of about two years, my circumstances got worse, partly through bad luck and partly because I was living with increasing dysregulation (and at that time, I did not know what this was). I suffered medical problems and complications that ultimately required 14 major surgeries. In the recession following the 2008 housing crisis, the clients who had employed me as a consultant all lost their jobs, leaving me with almost no work for over a year. I had few friends, and out of loneliness I made a terrible error of judgment by getting involved with a man who turned out to have a serious drug addiction. Just a few months into the relationship, he overdosed and died. I'm the one who found him.

This was the second-lowest point of my life, and one Saturday night while my kids were at their dad's house, I found myself lying face down on the floor, sobbing. I had no one to call and nothing to pray to. This was the moment I figured it out: All the time I was using the Daily Practice in the past, it was fixing something in me, and when I stopped doing it, I stopped being fixed. CPTSD symptoms now rolled through my life freely and ruined things.

I started writing and meditating again that night and began to recover quickly.

One morning after meditation, some thoughts came into my mind that went like this: I had gifts to bring to the world—intelligence and strength that couldn't get out because of my chaotic inner state and the messed-up people I seemed to attract. I was living my life feeling resentful and put-upon, believing I'd been passed over and cursed. But that morning after meditation, the truth was right in front of me. I was the one cutting me off from life's possibilities. The "curse" was something I was doing to myself.

What I needed became clear: I would have to step up and face reality, and do whatever it took, as quickly as possible, to overcome my self-defeating behaviors. I didn't know how I would do it, but I accepted this to be true.

What followed was the systematic transformation of my life through a process I put together by trial and error with the help of a few mentors, a dozen books, and a handful of small miracles. I became religious about my Daily Practice and prayed morning and night. I set about making practical changes quickly, taking care to eat well, sleep well, and dress well. With barely any social life, I had plenty of quiet time and used it to be more present with my kids and reflect on how to put our lives in order.

I started saying "I'm sorry" and "thank you" more often. I stopped arguing with my kids' dad, deleted all the sad, angry music from my playlists, and practiced refraining from negative talk.

I did still talk about my life, but I cleaned up the *way* I talked about my life. I tried not to talk about problems or negative feelings to just anyone, unless it was for their benefit. And I cut off connection to people I had dated in the past or people where there was a nonmutual attraction. I called them up or e-mailed them, explained the change I was making, and wished them well.

It was as if a big, bright window opened in a dark, stuffy room. I knew that no matter what happened, I would be okay.

About this time, I met the man who is now my husband. It was a *very* slow courtship, where he didn't even meet my kids and *nothing* happened in the first year. From the summer when we met until the wedding was more than five years, and that was about the right amount of time for me to really get to know him. Learning to trust that he really loved me and my kids was one of the harder things leading up to engagement, and it took time. But on January 18, 2014, we were finally married.

My kids were thriving. I was growing intellectually and having fun with new friends. I owned and ran a small but successful video-production company. But still, I'd wake up at 3 A.M. most nights, haunted by a feeling that I was meant for more—that the answer was so close, but I couldn't put my finger on it. I couldn't help feeling that my life was passing me by.

I was on the cusp of discovering my gifts.

WHAT ARE GIFTS?

You've probably heard this term. *Gift* refers to the unique abilities endowed to each person *specifically for the benefit of other people and the world.* It is a spiritual concept, sometimes referred to as a "calling," reflected in many of the world's faith traditions. Many nonreligious people also recognize instinctively that a greater "potential self" lives within each of us, capable of becoming much more than we are now if we can only overcome our limitations and access the greatness inside.

There are dozens of possible gifts, among them things like teaching, healing, music, leadership, and intuition. Some people have one gift; some have more than one.

Trauma can suppress your gifts and rob you of the opportunity to develop them, but healing trauma makes it possible to grow into them at last. I've come to believe that the deepest happiness we can have comes through finding, developing, and expressing our gifts.

Gifts are different from talents. Talents are fairly easy to recognize, but they're not necessarily for the benefit of the world. For example, I have an ear for language and an eye for correct grammar and punctuation—both talents that have (happily) helped me earn a living throughout my life.

Gifts can take time to manifest, and even when they are active, you might not recognize them as anything special. *The main sign of a gift is that other people benefit from something you do.* They will tell you outright that something that you said or did affected them positively. You might notice a pattern in comments like this from different people, pointing to a gift. Sometimes people won't express it to you directly, but you'll see that something good is happening for them because of you. For example, if you're a high school basketball coach whose influence on players results in many of them making positive transformations in their lives, your gift might be encouragement.

Here's something counterintuitive that you may discover: Just because you are good at something doesn't mean it's a gift. And just because something is a gift, it doesn't mean you are good at it (yet).

FINDING *YOUR* GIFTS

In the next section, I'll share with you a list of 20 possible gifts so you can start to consider what yours might be. Once you have an inkling of where your gifts might lie, your next step is to test them out, give them a try, and see what happens.

If it's a gift, using it will begin to change you for the better. You'll feel more fulfilled and less like life is passing you by. Though using a gift can be hard work and full of stress (like anything else), it tends to bring a sense of fun and excitement into your life, and the feeling that your life is going somewhere.

If something is not a gift, the telltale sign is that no one seems to benefit, and the work feels tedious and draining—or just something you do to earn a living. There's nothing wrong with that: Many people do one thing for work, while their gifts are expressed in other areas of their lives.

Everyone has individual gifts, and luckily, there is great variety. Sometimes when we come together as a group of friends, a working team, or a couple, our gifts complement those of one another or form a new, joint gift. My husband and I, for example, discovered as soon as we were dating that large groups of friends seemed to gather around us for conversation and dinner, though this didn't happen for either of us much before we met. Now, years later, hosting groups of people is still a highlight of our lives. He cooks, and I walk around helping everyone feel welcome. Many people going through hard times have found solace in our living room, and many lasting friendships have formed there. This joint gift is not a combination of our individual gifts—it's its own thing. We are very different people too. But our gatherings spring naturally from a creative chemistry we have when we're together.

Gifts reveal the truth in the saying "It takes all kinds of people to make the world go 'round." As people, we literally need each other to become fully ourselves. Collaborating with other people is often fraught before we've healed our trauma symptoms; the joy of working with others is one of the pleasant surprises that might lie ahead for you.

Possible Gifts

This list of 20 possible gifts is drawn from one of my advanced coaching programs and is inspired by a number of similar tools that are offered in both spiritual and secular contexts. I've adapted it for use by anyone, in hopes you'll find insight to guide your next steps in becoming who you really are.

Read through the gifts along with the characteristics listed under each one, and mark any that you think might be one of *your* gifts.

Teaching

- When I'm in a group that needs to learn something, I find myself jumping into the role of teacher more often than not.

- I'm often told that when I'm explaining something, I'm especially easy to follow and understand.

- I love teaching other people.

Healing

- I'm often told that my presence and/or care was a big part of someone's recovery from illness or injury.

- I feel most fulfilled when I can witness and support another person's healing.

- When someone I know is sick or injured, I find myself jumping into the role of caregiver.

Generosity

- When I see someone asking for money, I almost always stop and give what I can.

- It gives me great pleasure to share what I have (money, time, belongings) with people who need those things.

- Many people have benefited, in important ways, from the time, money, and things I've given them.

Inspiration

- When I encounter people who are cynical and/or seeking meaning in their lives, I tend to try and help them believe that transformation and good things are possible.

- I light up when I talk about the "forces of good" (or God) to other people.

- Many people have told me that when I've been in contact with them, it led them closer to a sense of meaning or of a higher power (God).

Encouragement

- I believe that each person has great potential, and I deeply enjoy helping them see, become, and do their best.

- When I see someone feeling like they're no good, I always want to show them all that they are capable of being and achieving.

- Many people have told me that speaking with me helped them to aim high and do good in ways they would not have otherwise done.

Hospitality

- My home is often full of guests and visitors.

- I love entertaining and creating loving and fun times for others.

- People who come to my home tell me they feel welcome and comfortable.

Comfort

- When I see someone in pain, making them comfortable is always my highest priority.

- I'm always the one who helps out sick friends or rescues injured animals.

- People often tell me that the way I care for them when they're sick or feeling sad makes them feel relaxed, safe, and loved.

Support

- I'm more comfortable supporting a leader than being a leader.

- When I'm near accomplished people and leaders, I have a desire to help them do great things.

- I've been praised many times for helping another person accomplish something big and important.

Creativity

- My creativity "sneaks" into nearly everything I do.

- It's a joy for me to use my creativity; I get "in the zone" and lose track of time.

- People have told me many times that my creative work has affected them deeply.

Organization

- When I work in groups, I find I'm most needed as an organizer or administrator.

- I thrive when I have the opportunity to plan my days and stay on schedule.

- In a project, I'm the person who is detail oriented.

Broad Knowledge

- The people in my life and/or in my work rely on me for my general knowledge; this is often how I serve groups in which I'm involved.

- I'm most happy and at peace when I'm learning (from books, classes, documentaries, podcasts, and videos, etc.)

- Whenever I have free time, I'm drawn to reading and learning.

Seeing the Big Picture

- It's a joy for me to discover how seemingly disparate things fit together.

- I'm frustrated when others are bogged down in details and would rather be discussing things like opportunities, possibilities, and a greater vision.

- I see things in the big picture that not everyone sees, and because of this, I've been useful to people and groups where I'm involved.

Speaking

- Speaking with people, including strangers, comes naturally to me.

- People have told me I have a way of describing things when I speak that helps them know and/or feel things (in a positive and constructive way) that had not been accessible to them before.

- I'm good at verbal communication and feel at ease speaking with individuals or groups.

Writing

- I get feedback that my writing has made a positive impact on people in some way.

- I'm a good writer.

- I write even when I don't have to write; it tends to calm me and help me think clearly.

Beauty

- I see the beauty in ordinary things and can't help but try to illuminate this for others.

- The people in my life feel joy in and are drawn to the spaces (rooms, gardens) where I've worked to make things beautiful.

- I delight in beautiful things, places, and environments.

Solitude

- I tend to feel unhappy when I don't get sufficient alone time.

- I feel most alive in solitude.

- I'm best able to be useful to other people by working alone.

Service

- I love when I work hard on a project and get to see what a positive impact my work has on others.

- I excel at seeing what needs to be done and doing it.

- I'm often the person behind the scenes who makes big events and complicated projects possible.

Leadership

- I gravitate toward situations where I can be in charge; I'm best able to contribute that way.

- There have been many instances in my life where my leadership made a large, positive difference in the outcome of a project or organization.

- I'm most comfortable in situations where I'm in charge.

Intuition

- I have ways of hearing and understanding people's troubles or needs that I'm not sure how I know (but that prove true).

- People tend to look to me to discern whether a new person or situation is good and trustworthy—or whether it's trouble.

- I trust my intuition more than any other form of perception.

Simplicity

- I come alive in situations where there are fewer options.

- I've helped others feel happier by enjoying life's little pleasures.

- I need very little in the way of material things to be happy.

FOR YOUR JOURNAL
• • • • • • • •

- Of all the things you do in your life, what gives you joy?
- What is it that causes people to tell you, over and over, that what you did made a positive difference for them?
- Read through the gifts again and put a second mark on gifts that give you joy, and a third mark where you've received frequent feedback that you've made a difference. The gifts with the most marks can be considered *your* "possible gifts."

WHAT HAPPENS NEXT?

Once you've identified three to five possible gifts, it's time to test the hypothesis that they really are your gifts. The only way to do this is by trial and error.

Some possible gifts on your list may fade from significance, while others—maybe just one of them, or maybe two or three—will gradually come into focus. You may notice a feeling of excitement about trying and developing them.

It takes time and sometimes courage to test your gifts. Let's say you've become the go-to person at work for people who need help installing software, and because so many people have appreciated your help, you think teaching might be your gift. Your next step is to create an opportunity to teach people something beyond what you already do—to stretch your wings a little bit, even if it means stepping beyond your comfort zone. You might volunteer to teach adult literacy at the library, offer a formal workshop at work, or (if you're a parent) teach your child to build a birdhouse.

Don't be discouraged if your efforts on one gift seem to go nowhere. The gift might be waiting for a different way of using it. Or it might not be your gift. But the only way you'll find out is by testing it.

When you do identify a probable gift and begin to use it the way it is meant to be used, there will be a sense of rightness, inspiration, and momentum. It may be subtle at first, but when you sense these things, keep pressing forward. As you get closer to your gift, you'll notice other aspects of your life becoming sweeter and more lively.

Your gifts will come into focus more strongly as you free yourself from old fearful and resentful thinking, and this is why the Daily Practice continues to be an important means of staying both strong and open to the changes unfolding in your life. Clearing away old habits and toxic relationships gradually brightens the light you shine on the world, and your "shine" makes it harder and harder for new problems to latch on to you.

As you begin to use your gifts, the signs of healing listed on pages 133–136 in the previous chapter will get stronger in you. Life will get easier for you, even though problems are part of life and you'll have some of those to face too. You'll grow in confidence that whatever happens, you'll be able to figure out what to do.

HOW I DISCOVERED MY GIFTS

I learned the idea of gifts from a priest who helped my husband and me to discern whether to get engaged. Then, early in our marriage, I went to see him about the "haunted" feeling, and he taught me about gifts and how a person finds them. He's the one who told me that one big sign of a gift is that people tell you over and over that something you do has a positive impact on them.

He asked if there was something in my life where I got that feedback. After thinking about it, I told him it was when I talked about my own healing, which was usually in 12-Step meetings. In a strong and definite way, people seemed to feel inspired by my story and wanted to take a step up in their lives too. So maybe the gift was inspiration, I speculated. That, and maybe writing. He suggested I give them a try.

A month later, my husband and I had a potluck dinner at our house. We hosted many of them in those days and often had guest speakers, but that night I appointed myself as the speaker and told the invitees I'd be telling the story of my healing. I invited the priest, and he was seated among the 40 or so guests who had packed in to hear me. I spoke for an hour about my life—the story you now know too, through this book. In the middle of the story, I stopped to take a sip of water and noticed the room was completely silent. I paused for a moment to look at everyone's faces. They were sitting straight up, completely still, waiting for the next thing I would say. I looked at the priest, and he smiled and nodded. This was the gift! All I had to do was keep using it and see where it took me. The rest, as they say, is history.

With all my heart, I encourage *you* to try out your gifts and look for the sign that tells *you* you're making a difference. We live in a world full of trauma-shaped holes, but now there is one less of them, because you are here, healing the wounds of the past, becoming your full and real self, and sharing your special and unique light with all of us at last, blessing the world as only you can.

APPENDIX

COMMON QUESTIONS ABOUT THE DAILY PRACTICE

Why Does the Daily Practice Help with Trauma-Related Symptoms?

One day soon I hope we'll have the benefit of formal, clinical evaluation of the Daily Practice techniques to better understand why so many of us experience dramatic healing with them. Until then, we can look to studies that show that writing about negative emotions and having a regular meditation practice are each effective at reducing trauma symptoms, and we can test the techniques on ourselves and determine for ourselves whether they are helpful.

When I first learned the Daily Practice, I learned it as a spiritual practice and was taught to write the fears and resentments as a prayer, with the word *God* at the top of the page, and then naming the specific fears and resentments that were bothering me and asking for them to be removed. I didn't believe in God when I first started, but I wanted to feel better, and I was willing to try what had worked for the friend who showed the techniques to me.

It worked quickly, definitively, and powerfully. So for many years, I attributed my healing to a mix of divine aid and common-sense effort. I still see it this way, in fact, even though strictly secular people can benefit from it too.

After more than a decade of faithfully writing and meditating twice a day, I experimented with *not* using the techniques (the embittered period I described in Chapter 9). At first nothing much changed, but within two years, my life was a mess in every way, so I picked up the pen and paper and started again. Within weeks, my mental and physical health improved, and my ability to be calm and focused returned. This helped me to experience directly the contrast of "me with the Daily Practice" and me without it.

In 2014, when the revolutionary research explaining neurological dysregulation was published, I immediately understood that "me without the Daily Practice" had become a nearly constant state of dysregulation. When I resumed the practice, I became re-regulated. So when I learned about dysregulation and complex PTSD, it made perfect sense to me.

That's when I also discovered the work of Dr. James W. Pennebaker, the social psychologist and professor emeritus at the University of Texas at Austin I mentioned earlier who researched the therapeutic effect of writing and developed a method known as "expressive writing."[1] In a series of studies over decades, his work demonstrated that writing regularly about feelings and thoughts not only helps one cope with emotional distress but has a marked positive effect on physical and mental health.

Writing is therapeutic, he believes, because it leads us to acknowledge and accept our emotions; to practice introspection; to express blocked feelings; and to make sense of traumatic experiences, integrating them into our life's story. He also posits that writing about trauma instead of talking about it offers us the freedom to be fully honest with ourselves without the (potentially inhibiting) influence of the person who listens to us when we talk about the same feelings.

For meditation in general, there is ample material online that documents its positive effects for healing the effects of trauma and healing the individual symptoms so many of us experience. I use Transcendental Meditation, for which there is copious research—and enough with sufficient rigor to safely say it is helpful for treating trauma symptoms.[2]

For you, the best test of how well the Daily Practice works is to try it and see what happens. I recommend using it exactly as taught—for seven days during which you are not using other techniques or trauma-healing modalities (including talk therapy), and just see if there is a difference. You can then make a decision whether to continue. These practices are simple and compatible with any other methods of healing that you may be using.

Why Do We "Sign Off" after Writing?

The sign-off is the most important part of writing the fears and resentments; it is why we take the time to name each fear and resentment with specificity. Without it, the Daily Practice doesn't work.

If you are just writing everything bothering you and *not* signing off, you'd basically be ranting on paper, which doesn't give you the lighthearted feeling you seek. There's a lot of evidence that ranting, hitting pillows, and venting about your stress and grievances is not therapeutic, and in fact these can retrigger you and amplify an already negative emotional state.

So we use a very specific writing format that allows you to name the fears and resentments for the purpose of releasing them. Or (if you believe in a higher power) asking them to be removed—in other words, as a prayer. The sign-off expresses a very specific intention to get free of the problems that hold you back today.

As I suggested in Chapter 3, you can think of your fears and resentments as wet leaves on the windshield of a car. You can't drive the car without removing them; you wouldn't be able to see where you're going! You don't need to examine them as you peel them off or know what kind of tree they came from. You just push them onto the street, get in the car, and drive. So the release statement could be paraphrased as, "I want this stuff off the windshield, because I want to go forward. And for that, I'll need to see."

What Should I Do with the Paper When I'm Done Writing?

When you're done writing, it's important to destroy the paper you used. I recommend doing that right away. The only exception is if you have a buddy (a person who also does the Daily Practice) and you have an arrangement that at some point later that day, you're going to read to them what you wrote. In that case, keep the paper in a safe place until you can read it, and *then* destroy it.

We do this because the writing is your safe and private place to express your most painful (and even shameful) thoughts—for example, an angry and fleeting thought that your best friend is an idiot (though in reality, you love her). So, if your friend were to read what you wrote, she'd be horribly hurt, not realizing that you do this writing to get those angry thoughts out of the way so you can remain true to how you really feel about her.

Sometimes, of course, we do feel someone is an idiot. This still goes on the paper and still should not be left lying around.

So shred, burn, dunk in oil, or ruin the paper in some way, and your secrets will remain safe.

In What Order Do We Write the Fears and Resentments?

There's no special order for writing fears and resentments. Just write them as they come to you, as a stream of consciousness. Keep in mind that when you hit a resentment, it's going to be followed by one or more fears, because the format is structured that way. For example, "I'm resentful at Joe because I have fear he punched me in the nose in second grade. Fear all the kids bullied me then. Fear it made me anxious until I was 30" (and so on). And then you might have a cascade of fears about *that*, and so you'll write what comes to you. Or you might have nothing more on that, and a new fear or resentment is now on your mind and headed for the page.

There's no need to be thorough about it all. You just write what happens to be agitating your mind. There's no need to capture all the fears of your life or all the fears on a particular topic. Just write what's on the surface now, and trust that what needs to be written will come soon or on another day.

What If I Keep Having the Same Fears and Resentments Each Day?

Repetitive fears and resentments are normal and to be expected. What happened to you in the past occurred in layers, and that's the same way it comes off sometimes. It looks like the same thing again and again, but just assume it's another layer that needs to go, and trust that one day it will be gone and you'll either forget about it or realize you want to do something about the problem that nags at you. When in doubt, you can write extra pages about your concern that you're doing it wrong and it's just the same old stuff.

Some topics that many of us write over and over about include fear that we're incompetent, fear we're not attractive, fear no one likes us, and fear we'll end up alone. We all have those fears, and because we are human, they're bound to come up over and over again. So don't even worry about it. Whatever is troubling your mind as you're writing, it goes on the paper.

What If Writing Fears and Resentments Causes Them to "Manifest"?

Many people have been trained that distressed thoughts should be pushed out of your mind and that expressing them will make them more real. But here's the thing: If you're having those thoughts and feelings, they've already manifested. Your willingness to write a thought on paper and ask it to be removed is therefore the means for you to "unmanifest" it. Poof. It's gone.

But What If My Fears and Resentments Are Real and Appropriate?

Okay, let's say you write, "I have fear there are snakes in the basement," and then you go get a flashlight and you discover there actually are snakes in the basement! Your fears and resentments might be large or small, appropriate or imagined. We don't worry about that. If it bothers you, put it on the paper. Sometimes after meditation a given fear or resentment will evaporate and you'll never think of it again. Sometimes it will recur for a while, and sometimes you'll come out of meditation clear that you need to do something about it. These are all good outcomes, and the Daily Practice helps you see your choices and sense what, if anything, you need to do. It can be (but isn't always) a way to access important insights and inspiration.

I remember I had fear when I was 30 that I never went to grad school, and I feared I was the sort of person who should go, and feared I was therefore missing out, making a mistake. One day I came out of meditation with a clear mandate in my mind: *I must go to grad school right now in public policy!* I took the day off from work and literally *ran* to UC Berkeley, arriving breathless and sweaty at the admissions office. The Public Policy School said the deadline for applications had passed a while ago, that preparing an application takes weeks, and hardly anyone gets in anyway. But you know what? I talked them into letting me apply (and it really was hard). This was February. And I didn't know how I was going to pay for it, but the day I got the acceptance letter, I also found out I had inherited a little sum of money that (with loans and part-time work) would get me through the first year. By fall, I was at my desk in the program.

So you might have fear that's prompting you to do something that is actually right for you. The fear presents itself; then you name it and get it out of the way so that you can think without fear about what you really want.

If you have fear that writing something down will make it manifest, write: "I have fear that writing my fears will make them manifest . . ." and then whatever the rest of the fears are. Ask for those to be removed. See what happens.

Remember, nobody must keep going with this Daily Practice if they don't like it or if it in any way conflicts with what they're trying to do in their lives. You get to decide if it's useful to you.

It has been my experience that using the Daily Practice reduces the bad things in my life and that gradually, there are fewer things to be fearful or resentful about. It's natural and can't very easily lead you astray.

Why Focus on Fear and Resentment, and Not All the Other Emotions?

Some people ask why we don't also write about jealousy or grief, for example. The answer is, we do write about them, but we lump them all into two buckets called *fear* (if they are anxious in nature) and *resentment* (if there is anger there). It's one of those things where it's easy to overthink it, but better not to do so.

A full range of emotions are your birthright, and you recovering them is part of your healing. But when you're doing the Daily Practice, you're not trying to get rid of *everything*. You're just trying to name the fearful and resentful thoughts that are bothering you right now, and ask for them to be removed. Many of us find that with less fear and resentment, we're more attuned emotionally, and the positive feelings like joy, acceptance, and gratitude naturally become stronger and more accessible.

When in doubt, just get it out. Call it a fear, even if the thought is about how excited you are that something good is happening later. If you get it wrong and put the thought in the wrong pile, don't worry, because this method knows what it's doing. You just do your best to name the fearful thoughts or resentments, ask for them to be removed, then meditate and see what happens.

Can I Modify the Daily Practice to Do It My Own Way?

Yes. You are in charge of your healing, the tools you decide to use, and how you'll use them.

That said, I recommend you try the techniques, exactly as taught, for a week. Write and meditate twice a day for seven days so that you can learn the rules before you break them. After teaching the Daily Practice to thousands of people, my experience is that the form really does matter. Your ideas for improving it might prevent you from experiencing the subtle power that can best be accessed by following directions.

If you already have an established meditation practice, that's probably the best kind of meditation to use, because it's automatic and easy for you.

If you are not a regular meditator, I'd suggest sticking with techniques that involve sitting down and not trying to accomplish anything other than resting. I would not recommend guided meditations (all that input will clutter your resting mind), nor walking meditation (lovely, but it has a totally different goal). Many people use mindfulness techniques, and those are fine, but try not to put too much effort into watching your breath or noticing your thoughts. In the Daily Practice, a light rest is what we're after.

What If I Feel Worse When I Do the Daily Practice?

Sometimes people tell me that they follow the instructions, but it makes them feel angry or frightened.

First, if writing and/or meditation doesn't feel good for you, it's okay not to do it. Maybe it doesn't suit you, or maybe in time it will work better for you.

In a few cases, people *really* feel terrible when they try to meditate; this can be an issue for those who are often dissociated, for example. It makes them feel destabilized. If this is you, you can just focus on the writing. Likewise, if it's the writing that bothers you, just do the meditation.

But usually, people who aren't yet feeling the benefits need only a little adjustment of technique. Here are the likely culprits:

The way you're writing resentments is missing the "because I have fear" part. Let's say you're resentful at your mother because she drank (this is the thought or feeling you're having). When you write, you don't say, "I'm resentful of my mom because she drank." Instead, you write, "I'm resentful of my mom BECAUSE I HAVE FEAR she drank." Then you can continue with other fears associated with that, or not—such as "Fear that affected me, fear I'll never find a good partner, fear I now have a damaged red-flag detector for drinkers . . ." and so on. The magic phrase is "because I have fear," inserted between the target of your resentment and the reason you resent them.

Inserting this is the key to why the writing works. But it's easy for people new to the technique to forget that. We put it there for two reasons: One is, you can never really be 100 percent sure about your perception. So we admit we have fear just for good measure.

The second reason we always insert "because I have fear" is that resentment is *made of* fear. Without fear, you'd be angry for a short time and forget about whatever was bothering you.

Now, let's say in this case, you know for a *fact* that your mom drank. This is a knowable thing, but we still write, "I'm resentful at my mom because I have fear she drank," (a) because we are open to the possibility our perceptions are not quite accurate, and (b) as an acknowledgment that fear mixed with anger festers into resentment. In other words, we are resentful because we have fear.

You don't do the Daily Practice regularly, or you don't meditate afterward. Regularity is important and brings benefits that are simply not available with an occasional practice. Remember, the Daily Practice isn't an aspirin; it's a toothbrush.

You try to get to the bottom of your fears and resentments rather than just let them come to you. Maybe you set a goal to cover a certain topic, or you try to list all the fears and resentments you've ever had, or try in any way to grab the steering wheel of this subtle process that works best when we let *it* run the show.

Allow the fears and resentments *come* to you. Don't dig for them. Then rest in meditation. Don't "try" to have an empty mind. Don't aim for any particular outcome except to feel better. Especially refrain from mixing it with a different approach to healing that involves, say, venting. The Practice is a humble act where we get honest about the troubled thoughts in our minds and seek with all our hearts to get free of them.

You don't do both techniques. If you shortchange yourself on the amount of writing or duration of meditation, this will diminish the results. You can go about a month with just writing. At about that point, though, it will start to "tip you over," making you grouchy and emotional rather than giving you the smooth-flowing emotional processing you need to keep going on this great adventure of healing trauma. We write so we can have enough calmness in our minds to meditate. And we meditate so we can rest enough to handle writing again the next time. Writing and meditating need each other.

What If the Daily Practice Inspires Me to Do Something That Turns Out Badly?

If you get the idea that you need to take action on something and then later realize that it wasn't a good idea, that's okay. You do the Daily Practice again, and you list your fears and resentments about that (and remember, you can be resentful at yourself, which we often are).

If you are using the Daily Practice twice a day, you can test your ideas freely and very rapidly sense if they are mistakes. This is a process you would normally have been practicing all through your youth; dysfunctional family dynamics and the resultant CPTSD symptoms can block you from learning through trial and error. This causes something that might be called a "developmental delay." Now you are free to catch up and learn at a healthy and even accelerated pace—trying things, making mistakes sometimes, apologizing or changing course, and then learning some more. If you become more open to trying new things, I especially encourage you to use the Daily Practice twice a day so there is always a way to process what you are learning and to detect any ways you may be about to make a misstep.

There will always be missteps, and life will always have problems. With the Daily Practice, you can face them with a clear mind and a readiness to take smart action.

Can the Daily Practice Work
If I'm Also Doing Talk Therapy?

Many people who are also working with a therapist have found the Daily Practice helpful. In fact, many therapists suggest that their clients use the Daily Practice between sessions so they can learn to calm triggers and develop more capacity for self-regulation.

Not all styles of therapy are perfectly compatible with a regular Daily Practice, however. If the approach is focused on talking to the clinician about distressed feelings and memories, and this person helps you reframe them or guides you to delve deeper into what happened, this could work at cross-purposes with the spirit of the writing and the meditation. The Daily Practice is something you manage yourself, and it involves *allowing* and *releasing* thoughts and feelings—not seeking them out, going deeper, or reframing them. In time, many people using the techniques experience a breakthrough, but this often comes *after* the realization that it's okay not to repeatedly talk about or go deeper into painful thoughts and feelings.

A breakthrough in the Daily Practice (and often in therapy) is likely to involve some frustration and resistance before you get there. When we're writing and meditating, there will be days when a buildup of fear and resentment feels like a dam will break, and we're scared to let that happen. But sometimes a breakthrough is waiting on the other side, when you find you have the inner resources to face and release even this. Mixing modalities creates the option of taking the path of least resistance by hopping back and forth between them. You should always do what feels necessary and right for yourself. But ask yourself if, by hopping around, you are avoiding facing the harder parts of the work that would help you move forward.

You can test the effect of the Daily Practice on yourself by using the techniques exactly as taught, twice a day, without leaving therapy; some people do this during the seven days between weekly therapy appointments. It can be valuable to test whether just the Daily Practice is enough. It can be freeing to discover that no person has to come in and fix it for you. *You* don't even have to fix it.

It can be good to experience how the techniques can change things (or you), where no person has to come in and "give" you the healing. Even *you* don't have to give you the healing. Solutions will come to mind in due time.

Do I Have to Do the Daily Practice Twice a Day?

No! You don't have to do anything you don't want to do. But if you want to experience what the Daily Practice can do for you, then yes, I recommend you do this twice a day—writing and meditating. The best time is first thing in the morning for the first one, and for the second one, some time at least six hours after that—maybe before dinner, and not too late at night. It has a beneficial effect that is nice to spread out through the day.

You don't just do it on bad days; you do it every day, which will help you get into the habit of doing it. There is something inside you that responds to the regularity of your practice. More insight will bubble up to the surface, and sometimes painful feelings; that's what happens when you start naming the things that are hurting you and making you anxious and angry. What's stuck begins moving, which sometimes brings tears but also keeps your healing moving, freeing you to be more yourself and to embrace life's experiences with less fear of overwhelm.

If it ever feels like too much, it's okay to stop or pause the Daily Practice until you feel ready.

Is It Okay to Do the Daily Practice *More* Than Twice a Day?

People who are in distress or who love this technique and what it does for them sometimes want to write and meditate more than twice a day. You can write as much as you like; I've been known to write in some very strange places—including while I sat in business meetings, pretending to take notes, because I was so distressed inside, I couldn't even think or listen. By writing a little bit, I could come back and be present in the meeting.

Write as much as you want. But I wouldn't meditate more than twice a day. That's a bit like checking out. One exception would be if you're sick, in the hospital, or in bed; then meditate all you like.

What If I Can't Stop Thinking When I'm Meditating?

Some people worry that if their mind wanders during meditation, they're doing it wrong. There are forms of meditation where rigorous focus and inner stillness are necessary, but this is not one of them. This is a restful meditation, and it's very forgiving. All minds like to think, and if you have CPTSD, you may have a lot of thoughts when you try to sit still. Don't worry about it too much. That's why we use a simple mantra like "Okay," or "This" as a little reminder.

My mind gets jumpy sometimes. I'll sit trying to meditate, and I'll remember an e-mail I forgot to send and get a great idea for my next video. In many forms of meditation, the goal would be to let the thoughts pass. But it's okay in Daily Practice meditation to keep a pad of paper next to you to jot down things you want to remember later, and then drop right back into meditation. Or let's say you hear an Amazon driver drop a package on your porch and you're worried it will get stolen if you leave it, and it's disturbing your meditation. It's okay to get up from meditation, take the package inside, then sit down to continue until the 20 minutes are up.

"Thinky" meditation is sometimes the result of too-little writing. So if you simply can't stop thinking, it's okay to stop meditating and do more writing until the 20 minutes are complete.

Can I Type My Fears and Resentments (on a Device) Instead of Handwriting Them?

If you have a condition that makes handwriting painful or impossible, typing your fears and resentments is fine. If you are unable to type, voice dictation is okay too. But if you are able, it's best to use a high-friction method of writing—the type you get with a pencil on paper as you drag the tip across it. The manual friction of writing communicates to your brain, and over time this becomes a positive trigger to begin releasing the negative thoughts and emotions.

There are times when getting your hands on paper and pencil is not possible. I remember telling Rachel once that I couldn't write because I didn't have a pen, but she was having none of that. She said, "When we want to get free we will write with blood on the wall!"

She didn't literally expect that, but I got her point. I learned that in any circumstance, I could make the motion of writing to get the fears and resentments out. Once when I was about to have surgery, as they wheeled me into the operating room, I wrote with my finger on the sheet (I had a lot of fear, as you can imagine), and I have subsequently used finger-writing on sheets to get back to sleep after a bad dream in the night. When I'm driving, upset or panicking about being late somewhere, I've written with my finger on the upholstery of the seat next to me. You can do this too. Just write the fears and resentments as you normally would, and be sure to sign off!

Once you're in the habit of writing with pen and paper, the very act of writing becomes a positive trigger to begin releasing negative thoughts and feelings on the spot.

Can Children Do the Daily Practice?

Yes. My kids first learned to write fears and resentments when they were about five years old to help calm them down for sleep. They had positive associations with it, because as toddlers they considered it a special treat to get to sit quietly on my lap while I wrote and meditated (we had a special red blanket they could bring to the chair, to remind them this was a time to be still and quiet). With children who are not yet able to write, you can teach them to tell you their fears and resentments while you take dictation. Then you write the sign-off with them and read back to them what they said, with a little praise and reassurance that naming those feelings and sharing them is a good, freeing thing to do.

Gradually my kids were invited to write and meditate in their own seats with grown-ups, though they tended to use these tools only when they were upset or anxious. One time, in the car with their dad (who also does the Daily Practice), they had a backseat fight so vicious he had to pull over to the side of the road, where he gave them pens and scraps of paper and refused to continue the journey until they wrote their fears and resentments (including the sign-off) and then shared them aloud.

Learning the technique helped the kids to express their fears and resentments around whatever it was they were fighting about. They got a chance to read aloud or (during their younger years) speak what was bothering them, and to be formally heard and supported to process those feelings. They learned a children's form of meditation from my teacher, Paul Brown, who suggests kids meditate one minute for each year of age (so, for example, a five-year-old can meditate for five minutes). Young children can usually best meditate by sitting down with their eyes open, saying a mantra quietly to themselves.

The Daily Practice works for kids the same as anyone, and when they're very young, they have the delightful advantage of being wholly open-minded about it, especially if you as a parent use the techniques every day and they've had the opportunity to see the subtle change in you afterward.

There's no need to pressure a kid to do it twice a day, but it can be a nice way to help them deal with intense stress or hurt feelings. One thing I loved with my kids is that once they had learned it, when they were having a hard time or something bad happened at school, or they had an argument or a bad dream, I could help them write, and then I would read back what they wrote. And because they were children and they were so trusting of me, they didn't even question whether it worked. I would just say, "Here, write your fears on paper. Ask for them to be removed. Is that better?" And they always felt better. It did not occur to them not to trust the process.

As children get a little older, it's important to be trustworthy. Ask if they'd like to read to you, but don't sneak and read their writing anyway if they say no. Don't use what they write to criticize or correct them, and don't use it as punishment, as it will take away the feeling of safety for them and could turn them off to the technique for a lifetime.

What If I Don't Have Fear and Resentment?

Sometimes people who are very new to the Daily Practice tell me they don't have any fear or resentment. Sometimes that's denial, or the mindset of someone who has been conditioned that it's not okay to have these feelings. But often it's a matter of how we define the words. Even animals have fear and resentment, and in the Daily Practice, we use these words very loosely.

"Fear" doesn't have to be something that scares you. For our purposes, it is any kind of anxiety or worry, or even a neutral thought that's knocking around in your mind when you sit down to write, such as "fear I'm hungry," or "fear I'm sad." You can throw those down with all the fears that are obviously fears, just to clear your mind and keep the technique simple.

Resentment is not just big, huge things where you have an ax to grind with someone. It can be anything that causes anger, from rage to mere irritation. It is resentment when you feel that things are unjust, not right, or ought to be different than they are, like the length of supermarket lines, the cost of health care, or "kids today."

If you sit down to write, thinking, *I don't think I have fears and resentments*, then write that: "I have fear I don't have fears and resentments." Do this twice a day until you do have fears and resentments. I promise you, they'll come to you soon enough!

Why Do We Call Everything "Fear"?

You might worry that it's foolish to call something a fear when it really *is* something frightening. So, let's say this month you couldn't afford to pay the rent, and you have fear you're going to get evicted. It's true—you might.

And you might have fear that if you write this fear and then release it or ask for it to be removed, you'll lose your motivation or ability to pay the rent, or you'll succumb to magical thinking and just "believe" it will be paid. But then, boom, it's not paid, and you get evicted.

Here's why releasing your fears isn't foolish at all: You have actual wisdom and strength at your disposal, and these are what help you face life's problems and find solutions. Your fear is neither wise nor strong; it's mental clutter that blocks you from direct access to the insight and impetus you need to handle problems.

Likewise, your resentment is not a boundary; it complicates your boundaries, causing you to lash out or turn angrily inward when the smart action might be to say no or fight back. People who were not taught or allowed to have boundaries as children often develop coping mechanisms to protect themselves, becoming resentful, avoidant, or people-pleasing instead of simply standing up for themselves and their own best interests.

Your fear and resentment are clutter in your mind that keep you from seeing exactly what you do need to do, what is rational and in your own best interest. You can't always see the red flags. You sometimes misjudge what's in your best interest, or you run out and do what's best for somebody else but not best for you. So just trust that if you can get your fears on paper and ask for them to be removed, what will be given back to you is (1) clarity, and (2) the power to act.

What If I Don't *Want* to Lose My Resentment?

Some people are at a stage of healing where they don't feel ready to have less resentment. They tell me that the reasons they're resentful are because of injustices so grave, it feels wrong to let the resentment go. They worry this is like pretending the bad things never happened, or that it's like forgiving something unforgivable. Sometimes the thought of having less resentment feels risky, as if there will be no protection from harmful people.

All these feelings are fine, and you can keep them or change them at a careful pace, if that suits you. This writing technique is for people who feel ready to have less fear and less resentment and who are interested in discovering what life would be like if that changed.

If you're not ready, you can still meditate if you like, and you can keep working on other aspects of your healing. If a day comes when your resentment feels more like a burden than something useful, come back and try the Daily Practice again.

I initially hesitated too. I had an attachment to my anger and resentment, using it like an electric fence to keep people from messing with me. I didn't yet have authentic boundaries, and that was the best I could do. But when I had less fear and resentment, I was able to construct good, useful, specific boundaries that I could actually employ—and I could deal with the surge of anxiety after stating my boundaries, which is common for people who are new to all this.

There's no need to get free of negative emotions. There's no need to forgive anybody. With time in the Daily Practice, you'll naturally become lighter hearted and experience waves of gratitude. Sometimes blessed forgiveness will land in your heart without you having to force it. There's no pressure to feel a certain way or to change. You can pursue good states, like being productive or grateful or accepting, or you can just allow them to come up like spring water that rises up in the well inside you as you keep healing, in your own time, the trauma-driven thinking and emotions that have been weighing you down.

What If the Meditation Feels Too Hard?

Childhood PTSD and dysregulation can make your mind feel like a bag of cats, so we don't usually just start meditating and experience complete bliss and stillness. Ha!

It's okay to come to meditation exactly as you are and give it a try. The fact that we write and release whatever fears and resentments are bothering us *before* we meditate can help a lot. It's genuinely okay if you keep thinking during meditation. Do your best and do the time (20 minutes). The results tend to be good no matter what it feels like.

I've been meditating regularly for most of the past 30 years, and I still get so "thinky" I sometimes forget I'm meditating and jump up and start doing something. When I remember (if that happens before my timer goes off), I sit back down and finish the meditation.

If you're trying to meditate but your mind is still busy with fear and resentment, stop meditating and do some more writing. And if that's all the time you have, let that be enough.

Now, one little caution: If you have a tendency to dissociate and/or meditation throws you into a feeling of terror or overwhelm, that's okay. You can stop and try again another time or set aside meditation as something that's not helpful for you.

How Long Will I Have to Do the Daily Practice?

When people ask me this, they are imagining that the Daily Practice will cure Childhood PTSD, and then they'll be done and can go on with life unaffected by past trauma forevermore.

Unfortunately, Childhood PTSD is only treatable, not curable. Most of us find that when we practice healing techniques and take good care of ourselves, we can get so much symptom relief that it sometimes *feels* as if we've been cured. But then we get careless with our Daily Practice, or something traumatic happens, and the symptoms return. So we know that Childhood PTSD is treatable, but it's always there.

This is why it's not a one-time practice; it's a daily practice. We do it in hard times and in happy times. We use it not like an aspirin (once in a while, if we feel we need it), but like a toothbrush: twice a day.

That said, you don't *have* to do the Daily Practice, ever; remember that. If you find it helps you, you will naturally return to it again and again, maybe even daily—and if you're lucky, for the rest of your life.

I write and meditate every day not because I'm self-disciplined, but because it feels good and it nourishes me. It changes the quality of my life, and I want that effect. I tried not doing it, and the results were miserable, but I needed that experience to know with certainty that the Daily Practice helps me profoundly. You may need that experience too: Try quitting, and see what you find.

Does the Daily Practice Conflict with Traditional Religions?

Writing and releasing (or asking for removal of) your fears and resentments, followed by restful meditation, does not conflict with any religious teaching.

The meditation technique I use (Transcendental or Vedic meditation), however, may not be suitable for people of certain faiths, especially if it's important in that faith to keep all spiritual and prayer activity grounded *in* the traditions of that faith.

If that's a concern for you, by all means, choose a form of meditation that's compatible with your faith. For example, in lieu of a mantra, some Christians who use the Daily Practice recite a short passage of scripture or a short prayer. If that's your preference, I suggest you choose something simple, not too goal oriented, and good for resting your mind. This is a time for rest, when you abstain from your usual efforts to improve yourself. There's a time to seek God's will for you and a time to let God's will be done for you. Let your meditation be the latter.

What If I Don't Have Time?

We are busy people, and many tell me they want to get better but don't have time to do the Daily Practice techniques. Let me tell you, I understand. For nine years, I was a divorced mother of two kids. And while my kids were young, life was hectic from the moment I woke up until the moment I fell asleep. I worked, and I was running around all the time between day care and work and home and errands, trying to get some edible food on the table, make the kids do homework, and then get them to school on time in the morning.

So, here's the question: What is time? *Time is the ability to pay attention, to use your mind to think and plan, and to take action at will.* When you're so stressed that you can't do these things, you'll waste a lot of time spinning your wheels and being caught in the rabbit hole of worry and rumination. You'll never feel that you "have time."

The Daily Practice takes about half an hour, twice a day. What you may find is that, rather than costing time, it reduces your stress and your mind is so clear that it *feels* as if you have more time than ever before. Rather than fretting and obsessing about things or scrolling mindlessly, you enjoy moments of peace and find you have the energy and clarity to take action as needed.

If you already get too little sleep, you may find that the meditation (especially if you get a teacher and learn a formal method) makes up for it. You might even fall asleep during meditation, which is not terrible. The form of meditation in the Practice, which takes 20 minutes, often feels as refreshing as a 45-minute nap.

Spending time on your healing is worth it, and of all the ways to heal, I believe the Daily Practice gives time back to you in the form of a rested and well-ordered mind.

What to Do with the Mental To-Do List

Sometimes when you're meditating, you'll be bothered by stray thoughts of things that you need to get done. *Oh my gosh, I forgot to call somebody!* Or, *Did I turn the stove off?* You may not need to stop your meditation right now, but for things you want to be sure to remember later, you can keep a pen and paper on hand to write what I call "intentions" *while* you're writing or meditating, or afterward.

A great blessing of the Daily Practice is that on some days it brings new ideas and important realizations throughout the day, but also sometimes *while* you're writing or meditating. This is a good thing! Go ahead and write these on your intentions sheet. If you like, you can keep it with you and read it and update it every morning.

How Can I Encourage Others to Do the Daily Practice?

Once you've had the experience, it's natural to want to share the Daily Practice with anyone who wants it—your partner, your sister, your employer, your clients, your friend who is struggling right now, and so on.

You can offer it to any person you think might benefit from it. Don't be surprised, though, if very few people are interested in it.

The one thing that seems to attract people to it is when they encounter a person who has changed for the better. As you continue to heal and change, people will ask you how you did it, and you can tell them—or refer them to this book.

I've learned never to push people to use the Daily Practice. I used to push and push loved ones to do it, and couldn't understand why they so stubbornly refused. I've learned over the years that when I'm pushing people, I'm basically criticizing them and believing I know better than they do what they need (and coincidentally, it's to be more like *me*!). But sometimes people are drawn to it, and they'll ask to be shown.

It feels good to witness a person with trauma symptoms just like I had emerge from that lonely, scared, and chaotic state into an easy alertness, with more power to connect with people. They seem to shine a little—with a light that was always hidden by the anxious mask they used to wear. At last you meet the confident person who is unafraid of whatever each day brings.

There's no need to pressure people to do this. Just use it yourself, as taught, twice a day. Let yourself *be* the change, and allow your gifts to shine your light for you, summoning those who are ready for you to share your wisdom with them.

Can I Do the Daily Practice with a Group?

Yes, you can do the Daily Practice with a group! Writing and meditating with others is a good way to deepen your practice and make friends who use the techniques too. When I have a party, I'll often invite those who write and meditate to come early so we can write and meditate together, which sets a peaceful and friendly tone for when the other guests arrive.

During the pandemic, many of us discovered that meeting over a videoconferencing platform like Zoom was not the same as meeting in person but pretty good anyway, with the added bonus that people all over the world could join us. On Zoom calls, it helps to have a timed session for the writing, followed by 20 minutes for meditation. In some meetings, we chat afterward; on others, we don't. Large groups benefit from meetings scheduled in advance, but you can arrange spontaneous, one-on-one "DP sessions" any time by pinging a friend when you're about to begin.

If you'd like to join the calls I lead twice a month, please visit **re-regulated.com** to see the current calendar. In my membership program, we also have a private online community where fellow members lead peer-led Daily Practice calls most days of each week, sometimes several per day. In these calls, you can get to know other participants and maybe find a buddy. This is someone who also does the Daily Practice and has agreed to hear you read what you wrote from time to time, usually on the phone or online.

Buddies are not therapists, and the person listening gives no advice. They merely serve as an encouraging witness and say things like "Good work. Thank you! I relate." You don't have to share everything you write. But sometimes it's helpful to share with another person what the fears and resentments are; it can often make them feel lighter and easier to release. Buddies sometimes have a one-way relationship (only one person reads), and some read to each other. Sometimes friendship forms, but it can also remain a strictly Daily Practice–related relationship.

Buddy relationships and Daily Practice groups are sturdiest when the focus remains not on trauma stories but on using the techniques together and supporting one another to change your lives for the better. The more regularly you practice, the more your healing blesses you, the people who write and meditate with you, the people you love, and even the strangers you encounter each day.

Everything bad that humans have ever done was driven initially by fear and resentment. These petty grievances, when left to fester, have a way of gaining momentum—like a train that heads only in one terrible direction. So each time your fears and resentments are released, you get off that train and become another person who brings a little more calm and goodness to the world for the benefit of all whose lives you touch, for your ancestors and your descendants, and for all men and women everywhere.

ENDNOTES

INTRODUCTION

1. Bessel van der Kolk, *The Body Keeps the Score* (New York: Viking, 2014), p. 47.

CHAPTER 1

1. Maercker et al., "Complex Post-Traumatic Stress Disorder," *Lancet* 400, no. 10345 (July 2022): 60–72, https://doi.org/10.1016/S0140-6736(22)00821-2.

2. "Study Finds Psychiatric Diagnosis to Be 'Scientifically Meaningless,'" NeuroscienceNews.com, July 8, 2019, https://neurosciencenews.com/meaningless-psychiatric-diagnosis-14434/.

CHAPTER 2

1. Bessel van der Kolk, *The Body Keeps the Score* (New York: Viking, 2014), p. 43.

2. Stone et al., "Response to Acute Monotherapy for Major Depressive Disorder in Randomized, Placebo Controlled Trials Submitted to the U.S. Food and Drug Administration: Individual Participant Data Analysis," *BMJ* 378 (August 2022): e067606, https://doi.org/10.1136/bmj-2021-067606.

3. Peter Simons, "Antidepressants No Better Than Placebo for About 85% of People," *Mad in America*, August 15, 2022, https://www.madinamerica.com/2022/08/antidepressants-no-better-placebo-85-people/.

APPENDIX

1. Chiara Ruini and Cristina C. Mortara, "Writing Technique across Psychotherapies—from Traditional Expressive Writing to New Positive Psychology Interventions: A Narrative Review," *Journal of Contemporary Psychotherapy* 52, 23–34 (2022), https://doi.org/10.1007/s10879-021-09520-9.

2. David Lynch Foundation Center for Resilience, "Selected Research on Transcendental Meditation as a Medical Intervention for Numerous Physical and Mental Health Conditions," June 7, 2023, https://www.davidlynchfoundation.org/pdf/Research-on-TM.pdf.

RESOURCES

This book is just the beginning of all the tools and support available through my online community, Crappy Childhood Fairy. Please visit the page just for readers like you, where you'll find news and stories from people who have used my healing method, plus downloads, videos, and links to all my courses, webinars, Daily Practice calls, coaching programs, and live events.

Visit: **re-regulated.com/resources**

You can also find my work online and on social media:

 crappychildhoodfairy.com

 YouTube youtube.com/c/CrappyChildhoodFairy

@crappychildhoodfairy

INDEX

A

abandonment, 15–16, 76, 125

abandonment mélange, 15

ACE study, 9–11

addictions. *See also* self-defeating behaviors

    to media and entertainment, 126, 134

    prevalence of, 17

    problems associated with, xv

    self-defeating behavior of, 125–27

    to substances, 125–26

    trauma and, 96

alternative treatments, 30–34

amygdala, 36

Anda, Robert, 9

anger

    attachment to, 168

    de-escalating, 117

    resentment as, 42–43, 166

    restraint of pen and tongue, 91

anxiety, 13, 16

apologies, 117–19

attachment, xv, 167–68

attentive care, 67–68

avoidance, 16, 110–11, 124, 128–29, 135. *See also* isolation

B

beauty in ordinary things, seeing, 146

behaviors and feelings. *See also* emotions; self-defeating behaviors

    changing one's, 130–32

    disconnected from, 101

belonging, struggling with, 109–10

black-and-white thinking, 125, 133

blame, 124–25, 134

The Body Keeps the Score (van der Kolk), xvi

body neglect, 124, 133

body-based therapies, 32–33

boundaries, 46, 96, 113, 115–16, 135, 167–68

brain development, 18

brain fog, 27

brain therapies, 30–32

brainspotting, 32. *See also* eye movement desensitization and reprocessing

broken connections, 111–12

buddy relationships, 173

Burchard, Brendon, 84

C

calling. *See* gift(s)

career. *See* work life

childhood trauma. *See also* complex post-traumatic stress disorder

    acknowledging, 21–23

    cause of, 6

    cognitive difficulties from, 16–17

    correlates, 9

    CPTSD vs., 3

    disconnection and (*See* disconnection)

    dysregulation and (*See* dysregulation)

    effects on nervous system, 18–19

    emotional relapse, 95

    feeling different from others, 105–6

ACKNOWLEDGMENTS

Thank you to my husband, Rob Clayton, and my sons, Harry Fricker and Jack Fricker. You are the family I always needed, and your love and support made it possible to finally write this book.

Thank you to Rachel Hope, for saving my life that night in 1994.

Thank you also to my parents, Barbara Azevedo and Bret Runkle, my stepfather Bill Azevedo, my godfather Per Fjeld, and my grandparents Marie Flotten, Ed Flotten, and Anna Marie Runkle. The chain has been broken, and I hope you are proud and feeling free at last.

Thank you to family members who have been especially supportive, including Esteban Azevedo and Natalie Cardot, Tim Fricker, Ann Fricker, and Joanna Gould and Richard Gould.

Thanks also to a few especially loving friends including Zack Alexander, Maya Dorn, Mary Fjerstad, David MacLeod, Chris Notti, and Eva Marie Notti.

Thank you to the people who have worked with me on Crappy Childhood Fairy, pouring intelligence and heart into everything they do, including Cara Alexander, Daphne B., Carol Fay Clark, Gabe Echeverria, Frida Engman, Monica Fulton, Jenny Geddes, Stephen Higginbotham, Gunvor Langeland, Ami Lin, Julie M., Kaki Mukhtar, S. Piza, Calista Sperry, Ashley Hannah Subramanian, Ramon Wickham, and Nika Zusin.

Thank you to the teachers and mentors who shaped my heart and my mind, including Paul Brown, Brendon Burchard, Evan Carmichael, Bill Golove, Fr. Dominic David Maichrowicz, O.P., and Fr. Michael Sweeney, O.P. Thanks also to the teachers in my childhood, especially Emily Booher, Gary and Gail LaBonte, and James Talmadge—and though I never met them, Fred Rodgers and Laura

Ingalls Wilder for the sanctuary and guidance their works provided to me as child.

And finally, a big thank-you to the people who helped to bring this book into the world, including my agent Iris Blasi from Arc Literary, and the wonderful team at Hay House, including my editor Anne Barthel, Bryn Starr Best, Tricia Breidenthal, Kirsten Callais, Julie Davison, Patty Gift, Allison Janice, Nusrah Javed, Lizzi Marshall, Lindsay McGinty, Monica O'Connor, and of course, Reid Tracy. Thanks also to the team at Nardi Media, who helped to get the word out, and Jasmin Singer and Erica Nielsen, who helped me find the right agent to begin this journey.

How lucky I am to have all of you in my life!

ABOUT THE AUTHOR

ANNA RUNKLE is the creator of the Crappy Childhood Fairy healing method, a breakthrough approach to help men and women everywhere heal trauma symptoms and change their lives—whether or not they have access to professional help. With more than a million subscribers to her YouTube channel, blog, courses, and coaching programs, she teaches the principles and techniques she originally developed to heal her own Childhood PTSD symptoms. Her method includes simple, self-directed exercises to calm emotional triggers and neurological dysregulation, to form caring relationships, and to change the self-defeating behaviors that are common for people who have lived much of their lives dysregulated. She lives with her husband and two sons in the San Francisco Bay Area.

Learn more about Anna Runkle and Crappy Childhood Fairy at:

CRAPPYCHILDHOODFAIRY.COM

Find free tools, real stories, videos and news about this book at:

RE-REGULATED.COM/RESOURCES

Hay House Titles of Related Interest

YOU CAN HEAL YOUR LIFE, the movie,
starring Louise Hay & Friends
(available as an online streaming video)
www.hayhouse.com/louise-movie

THE SHIFT, the movie,
starring Dr. Wayne W. Dyer
(available as an online streaming video)
www.hayhouse.com/the-shift-movie

✦ ✦ ✦

*THE GREATNESS MINDSET: Unlock the Power of Your Mind
and Live Your Best Life Today,* by Lewis Howes

*HAPPY DAYS: The Guided Path from Trauma to Profound Healing
and Inner Peace,* by Gabrielle Bernstein

THE HIGH 5 HABIT: Take Control of Your Life with One Simple Habit,
by Mel Robbins

*HIGHER PURPOSE: How to Find More Inspiration, Meaning,
and Purpose in Your Life,* by Robert Holden

All of the above are available at your local bookstore,
or may be ordered by contacting Hay House (see next page).

✦ ✦ ✦

NOTES

• • •

NOTES

• • •

We hope you enjoyed this Hay House book. If you'd like to receive our online catalog featuring additional information on Hay House books and products, or if you'd like to find out more about the Hay Foundation, please contact:

Hay House LLC, P.O. Box 5100, Carlsbad, CA 92018-5100
(760) 431-7695 or (800) 654-5126
www.hayhouse.com® • www.hayfoundation.org

———

Published in Australia by:
Hay House Australia Publishing Pty Ltd
18/36 Ralph St., Alexandria NSW 2015
Phone: +61 (02) 9669 4299
www.hayhouse.com.au

Published in the United Kingdom by:
Hay House UK Ltd
The Sixth Floor, Watson House,
54 Baker Street, London W1U 7BU
Phone: +44 (0) 203 927 7290
www.hayhouse.co.uk

Published in India by:
Hay House Publishers (India) Pvt Ltd
Muskaan Complex, Plot No. 3,
B-2, Vasant Kunj, New Delhi 110 070
Phone: +91 11 41761620
www.hayhouse.co.in

———

Let Your Soul Grow

Experience life-changing transformation—one video at a time—with guidance from the world's leading experts.

www.healyourlifeplus.com